CRITICAL ACCLAIM

"Patricia Spadaro is a marvelous guide through the inner realms of the heart. I always feel uplifted by her words."
—*Marianne Williamson, #1* New York Times *bestselling author of* A Return to Love

"*Honor Yourself* is more than just food for the soul—it is true healing for the heart. Patricia Spadaro provides an honest approach to self-love that will help us overcome the mental and emotional roadblocks that have created imbalances in our lives today. . . . She is a new voice to be reckoned with as a pioneer in healing."
—*Ann Louise Gittleman, Ph.D. C.N.S.,* New York Times *bestselling author of* The Fat Flush Plan *and* Before the Change

"A tightly woven guide to achieving inner peace."
—*Publishers Weekly*

"With stories from the wisdom traditions of East and West, personal anecdotes, and the experiences of contemporary people as they explore the art of giving and receiving, Spadaro illuminates ways to celebrate one's gifts and greatness, to appreciate the wisdom of the heart, set adequate boundaries, recognize and deal with unhealthy relationships, and honor necessary endings. . . . Engaging, compassionate, and at times, surprising."
—*ForeWord magazine*

"A compendium of insight, advice, and practicality within the context of modern life, *Honor Yourself* is highly recommended for personal self-help, self-improvement reading lists as being especially 'user friendly' and 'real world' oriented for establishing and maintaining mentally, physically, and spiritually appropriate balances between the needs of others and the needs of oneself."
—*Midwest Book Review*

"Having the ability to balance the needs of life, family and a career are always a challenge. This book shows us how to embrace our feelings, recognize the paradox of life and embrace the acceptance and support that is all around us."
　　—*Awareness Magazine*

"Rarely does a debut solo work of nonfiction explode on the scene with such deftness and clarity. . . . What makes any book great, from Dostoyevsky to Tolle, is when the reader pauses every so often to ponder what he has just read. This is just what I found myself doing from chapter to chapter."
　　—*ReverseSpins.com*

"Offers wise counsel on giving birth to your best self."
　　—*Frederic and Mary Ann Brussat,*
　　　SpiritualityandPractice.com

"Patricia Spadaro's book is essential reading. In searching the wisdom of our planet from the oldest truths to the most modern sayings, Patricia extinguishes the fires of myth that have held us in bondage to tension and stress. . . . Her writing is a breath of fresh air."
　　—*Chris Prentiss, author of* Zen and the Art of Happiness *and* Be Who You Want, Have What You Want

"Patricia Spadaro's elegant writing takes us exactly where we need to be, on the journey inward. . . . A must-read for everyone who struggles with balance: executives, stay-at-home moms, politicians, celebrities, and anyone who works hard and wants to live fully."
　　—*Iris Martin, psychotherapist and author of* From Couch to Corporation, The President's Psychoanalyst, *and* Mortgage Wars

HONORYOURSELF

HONORYOURSELF

The INNER ART of GIVING and RECEIVING

Embracing the power of paradox in your life

PATRICIA SPADARO

THREE WINGS PRESS

For information, address:

Three Wings Press
410 Fieldstone Drive
Bozeman, MT 59715
E-mail: info@threewingspress.com

For foreign and translation rights, contact Nigel J. Yorwerth.
E-mail: nigel@PublishingCoaches.com

Library of Congress Control Number: 2008910202

ISBN: 978-0-9816033-0-8

10 9 8 7 6 5 4 3 2

Cover design: Roger Gefvert
Interior design: James Bennett

The names and some details of the stories used throughout this book have been changed to protect the privacy of those who have shared their lessons on life's path. The information and insights in this book are solely the opinion of the author and should not be considered as a form of therapy, advice, direction, diagnosis, and/or treatment of any kind. This information is not a substitute for medical, psychological, or other professional advice, counseling, or care. All matters pertaining to your individual health should be supervised by a physician or appropriate health-care practitioner. Neither the author nor the publisher assumes any responsibility or liability whatsoever on behalf of any purchaser or reader.

CONTENTS

PART FOUR
CELEBRATE YOURSELF AND
HONOR YOUR OWN VOICE

———————— ❧ ————————

FOR SELF-REFLECTION
KEYS TO THE BALANCING ACT

*To the sages of East and West,
who have taught me that the greatest gift
I can give anyone is the gift of myself*

PART ONE

FILL YOURSELF *and* HONOR YOUR INNER NEEDS

You can look the whole world over and never find anyone more deserving of love than yourself.

—THE BUDDHA

While we are called to give, and to give joyfully, life also beckons us to master the art of balance. We have a duty not just to give to others, but to give to ourselves—and to see ourselves as worthy of receiving. We have a duty to honor others *and* to honor ourselves. What makes it so hard? We've inherited deep-seated myths about giving that keep us tied up in a lopsided approach to living. It's like trying to walk a tightrope in a straitjacket; we're not free to move a little this way or that to regain our balance. There is a way out of the dilemma, a way beyond the myths to the magic of honoring ourselves. It begins where all wisdom starts—through the door of paradox.

CHAPTER 1

THE PLAY *of* PARADOX

Do I contradict myself?
Very well then I contradict myself,
(I am large, I contain multitudes.)
— WALT WHITMAN

Life is rarely, if ever, an either/or equation. In principle and in practice, life is full of contradiction—paradox. It is a balancing act between competing tensions that vie for our time, our energy, and our attention, trying desperately to convince us that we must choose one over the other.

We are faced with these dilemmas every day. Should we spend more time with our family or building a career? Should we experiment and take risks or do things the way they have always been done? Do our children need more freedom or more control? Should we move away from home or stay close to our loved ones? Is it better to collaborate or to compete? Manage or mentor? Go it alone or get support? Be generous or draw boundaries? Stay quiet or fight back?

Chose what is most important to you. Not Everyone else.

According to ancient traditions, tensions are not only a natural part of life—they *are* life. The dynamic tension of opposites is exactly what gives birth to and sustains the ever-changing and ever-evolving elements of our universe. The interaction of opposites—symbolized in the swirling black-and-white circle of the T'ai Chi—exemplifies the universal principle that without one part of the pair, the other cannot exist.

Both sides of the picture complete the circle of wholeness. We must have both day and night, masculine and feminine, movement and stillness, right brain and left brain, the details and the big picture, focus and flexibility. Without the dynamic interplay between these powerful pairs, there is only stagnation, decay, and eventually death. Creative tension, or what I call the play of paradox, is absolutely essential for life and growth.

THE GOLDEN THREAD

What is paradox? A paradox involves two elements, truths, principles, or perspectives that seem contradictory but are both true. "It was the best of times and it was the worst of times," "all good leaders are servants," and "the more you learn, the more you realize how little you know" are all paradoxes. Much of the mystery and meaning, the comedy and tragedy of life are based on paradox. Its most ardent champions are scientists (who are still trying to solve the paradoxes of physics), comedians (who make a living pointing out life's everyday inconsistencies), and mystics, who believe we can glimpse the spiritual world while walking in the physical, the greatest paradox of all.

The sages of East and West speak often of what it is like to be caught inside a paradox. They describe it in ways that challenge us to move beyond our narrow thinking. They tell us that life's competing tensions are not contradictory but complementary, not mutually exclusive but mutually inclusive. Life, they say, is not a matter of this *or* that, but a matter of this *and* that.

Paradox is woven like a golden thread through the world's spiritual traditions. Saint Francis, for instance, pointed to paradox when he said, "It is in giving that we receive, . . . and it is in dying that we are born to eternal life." The Buddha told his students that taking refuge in the sangha (the community) was vital to their spiritual growth, but he also cryptically advised, "Look not for refuge to anyone besides yourselves." Lao Tze, the Chinese sage and founder of Taoism, taught, "To be empty is to be full. . . . To have little is to possess," and Jesus warned, "Be ye therefore wise as serpents *and* harmless as doves."

Were these great teachers just confused? Did someone make a mistake when they translated their words? Not at all. In the writings and in the lives of the wise ones, paradox permeates. In fact, one of the major lessons they have come to teach us is that we cannot ignore or chase away the tension of opposites, because that is how the universe operates. The Sufi mystic Rumi summed it up when he said that God "teaches by means of opposites so that you will have two wings to fly, not one."

Paradoxes are here to stay. *We cannot run from them; we can only embrace them and become one with them.* For, in reality, the apparent opposites are two sides of the same coin that are meant to reside in harmony.

The principle of paradox is nondenominational. No matter what background we come from or tradition we espouse, we will confront it. Our job, say the sages, is to learn to flow with the cadences of life as the universe asks us to bring first one and then the other side of the paradox to the fore in our lives at the right time and the right place. As an enlightened pundit once said, "Blessed are the flexible, for they shall not be bent out of shape."

CREATING BREAKTHROUGHS, NOT BREAKDOWNS

What happens when we don't embrace both sides of the paradox? Rather than creating breakthroughs, we create breakdowns. If we refuse to honor our physical needs, our body may shut down and send us to a hospital bed so that we are forced to listen. If, on the other hand, we give all of our attention to our material needs and don't nourish our spirit, our soul begins to ache and we may fall into depression without realizing why. In short, when we are out of balance, we become lopsided. It's like sitting at one end of a seesaw that suddenly flops down when our playmate runs off and leaves us alone; we hit bottom because there is nothing on the other side to create movement.

I believe that the greatest cause of stress is our inability to recognize and participate in the play of paradox. What often keeps us stuck on one side of the paradox or the other are the myths we have been taught and grown comfortable with. We don't even know that they are myths because we automatically accept them as true. They are based on assumptions we have made about the way the world works, and, like straitjackets, they prevent us from turning around to see the other side of the equation. They make us believe that we have no other options.

When we get out of balance, life sends its messengers—in the form of circumstances, people, and events—to help us get back into balance. It is human nature, of course, to want to run in the other direction, even to "kill" the messengers, so we don't have to hear the message. But that never works. The messengers just keep on coming until we stop and listen and accept their invitation to dance.

This book explores one of the many paradoxes of life—the paradox of giving and receiving. We are called to master the delicate dance of giving and receiving in virtually every area of our lives. You'll meet it when you deal with issues of abundance,

(handwritten margin note:) What has a man gained if he has all the possessions and loses his soul?

self-worth, health, relationships, career, and uncovering what your real gifts are, to name just a few. At its core, the paradox of giving and receiving deals with the overriding issue that challenges so many of us: *How do I balance what others need with what I need? In order to give to others, do I really need to give up myself?*

And NOT First Giving

At the outset, I should make it clear that honoring yourself is *not* about pampering yourself. And it's not about turning your back on those who need you. The issues surrounding giving and receiving are deeper. Much deeper. By honoring yourself, you are respecting, appreciating, and giving birth to your best self so you can give creatively—and abundantly—in ways that honor others.

While modern society is ill-equipped to bring us back into balance, the sages of East and West are experts. Throughout these pages, you will discover their practical, and often surprising, advice for mastering the inner art of giving and receiving. You will learn to recognize the myths that have held you hostage—myths that, like blinders, keep you from living a life filled with possibility and passion. You'll learn what it means to celebrate your gifts and greatness as you explore the inner dynamics behind giving with the heart rather than the head, setting boundaries, being honest about the unhealthy people in your life, using your feelings to stay true to yourself, finding your own voice, and honoring endings. Most importantly, you'll learn the steps for staying in balance. For when you learn the steps, you can perform the dance—and that's when the magic begins.

GETTING BACK IN RHYTHM

We're all in dance class, learning to master one move or another. We're all students of life, learning new ways to move in harmony with the cadences of life's ever-changing music. In our own ways, we're all teachers, too, as we share with others what we are learning. And, yes, it's paradoxically true that we do often teach what we most need to learn. With all the topics I've taken up for the books I've worked on, I have found this to be the case, and this one is no different. I am learning every day what it means to honor myself, my best self.

Depending on the day and the dance, I still stumble and get out of sync. I still have to stop, take a few deep breaths, and get back in step with the rhythm of the music. But I'm learning, and that's what counts to those incredibly patient instructors who coax and sometimes drag me onto the dance floor. I'm certain that I will get better at the dance as I practice, but I also know that I will always be learning. I will always be mastering new steps for honoring and celebrating my gifts.

So, in true paradoxical style, you could say that I wrote this book for you *and* for me. In part, it reflects my own journey and the discoveries I felt were so valuable that I had to share them with you. No book has all the answers or can teach you all the moves, but I hope this one will help you make more sense of life's twists and turns. I hope it will show you how to keep your step a little lighter when life sweeps you off your feet. And I hope it will help you smile and relax a bit more so you can simply enjoy the dance.

Some people would Rather Live in the shadows And hide. Excuses Like: That is just me, I've Never done that, I tried And it didn't work; And as a Result they Never move Beyond where they are. I'm sure each person Fell when they started learning to walk But didn't quit Trying until they learned to walk.

CHAPTER 2

SEEKING BALANCE

When one is out of touch with oneself,
one cannot touch others.
— ANNE MORROW LINDBERGH

"I am good when I give to others. It's better to give than to receive." Myth or magic?

Although many of us have grown up believing that it is our solemn duty to give, give, and keep on giving to others, that is only a half-truth—a myth that prevents us from living joyfully and giving fully. Instead, consider what the world's great sages say: *You have a duty to give to others* and *to give to yourself. When you are in need, you must also receive.* This advice sounds obvious, but how many of us are even near the top of our own copious to-do lists?

The principles of giving and receiving that apply to our daily lives are no different than the principles that operate in nature all around us. "A field that has rested gives a bountiful crop," said the Roman poet Ovid. The

But you must be open to receive

earth must receive enough sunshine, water, and nutrients before it can produce a bountiful harvest from the seeds we plant. After the earth has given birth to the harvest, it must then rest and restore its life force so it can give again. The same is true of your life. How can you give to others if you don't first nourish and fill yourself?

In a way that you might not have considered before, that question is embedded right inside the first principle we are taught as children—the golden rule. The golden rule is found throughout the world's traditions. The Mahabharata, the ancient epic of India, says, "Do naught unto others which would cause you pain if done to you." Islam affirms that a true believer "desires for his brother that which he desires for himself," and Christianity teaches, "Love thy neighbor as thyself." Yet, if we are to love and treat others *as* (that is, *in the same way that*) we love and treat ourselves, how does that leave them if we treat ourselves with anything less than love and affection? Put another way, we can't really honor others if we don't first honor ourselves.

MYTH:
It is always my duty to give to others.

MAGIC:
It is my duty to give to myself as well as to others.
By giving to myself, I am giving to others.

Here, then, we meet the first paradox of the inner art of giving and receiving—*we are able to care for and love others best when we care for and love ourselves first.* Like all true paradoxes, the two seeming opposites are not mutually exclusive but mutually inclusive.

There is a season for both giving and receiving. Ecclesiastes, known as "the Teacher," tells us (in the words made popular in the song by Pete Seeger): "To every thing there is a season, and a time to every purpose under the heaven: A time to be born, and a time to die; a time to plant, and a time to pluck up that which is planted; . . . A time to cast away stones, and a time to gather stones together; a time to embrace, and a time to refrain from embracing." Our job is to recognize which season we are living in at the moment and honor its call.

LEARNING TO GIVE TO YOURSELF

Some of us are awesome givers but not very good receivers. We don't ask for support. We don't admit to others or to ourselves that we need any. We don't even like to accept compliments. We reside on one side of the paradox ("I have a duty to give to others"), but we have forgotten about its complement ("I have a duty to give to myself"). When that happens, the universe will step in to wake us up, to create balance, and to show us that we must honor ourselves too.

No matter who we are, life automatically apprentices us to the art of giving and receiving, and our lessons often begin with what we can see and touch—our bodies. They start with the questions: *Do you love yourself enough to honor your body's needs? Do you give yourself the nourishment, rest, and recreation you deserve?*

If you don't willingly give that to yourself, your body will eventually make sure you get it. I saw this happen to an acquaintance I would spend time with a few times a year at business meetings. At one meeting, I asked how she was feeling, knowing that she had been recovering from a recent surgery. "I'm good, but busy again," she said with a frown. "If I don't get some time off soon, I'm going to have to schedule another visit to the hospital!" My heart skipped a beat as I realized that she might very well fulfill her own prophecy. She hadn't learned the lesson her body had tried to teach her the first time.

I'm no stranger to these lessons myself. When I was recuperating from my own unexpected trip to the hospital, a friend who was a nurse insisted on dropping by a few times a day to make sure I had everything I needed. She could see I was having a hard time sitting still and accepting the fact that I should rest, so she appointed herself my guardian angel for the week. I kept telling her that I felt fine and there was no reason I couldn't get up. Besides, there were so many things I needed to attend to. She didn't buy it. Looking me straight in the eye, she said, "Your job now is to sit still and relax."

She went on to tell me that she was just passing on a lesson she had learned when she had gotten sick. Like me, she had wanted to bolt from her bed and get going. A mentor of hers, catching her out of bed, sent her right back under the covers. "It's where you belong," she had told her. "You've been a nurse for so long that you think you should always be giving to others. Now you have to learn to receive." I could identify with that. I suspected that my tendency to work so hard for so long was partly what put me into the hospital in the first place. After my friend left, I sat back, closed my eyes, and promptly fell asleep. She was right. My body wasn't quite ready to start giving again.

Although we have been taught to think that spirituality encourages us to turn our attention away from the body and the material world to what is "otherworldly," there's a misconception wrapped up in that logic—a misconception that the world's great teachers have warned us to watch out for. They tell us that if we want to get in touch with our inner potential, we must also care for our bodies.

Rabbi Nachman of Bratslav, for example, said, "Strengthen your body before you strengthen your soul." More than two thousand years earlier, this same realization prompted the founder of Buddhism to develop one of the keystones of his philosophy—the Middle Way. Siddhartha Gautama, an Indian prince, left his wife and young child looking for something more than riches and material pleasure. For six years he was an ascetic, believing that the practice of intense austerities would lead him to his goal of becoming enlightened. Depriving himself of the nourishment he needed, he became so weak that one day he almost died of starvation.

Fortunately, a young girl found Gautama and offered him a bowl of nourishing rice milk. Realizing that his sacrifices and severe practices had not brought him closer to enlightenment, he gratefully ate the meal. Strengthened, he vowed to meditate under a tree until he attained enlightenment. Gautama faced many temptations during the ordeal but, with his strength intact, he succeeded at last in achieving his goal. After his awakening, the first thing he taught was that only when we walk the Middle Way—avoiding the extremes of both self-indulgence and self-denial—can we attain enlightenment, indeed any deeply held goal.

That universal principle of the balanced Middle Way applies as much to us today as it did to those who first heard it from the Buddha's lips. We, too, must examine whether our extreme sacrifices and the habits we think are making us "good" are actually bringing us closer to the fulfillment and meaning we seek in life. Do you sacrifice the needs of your body because you have adopted the myth that "my one and only duty is to give to others"? Do you ignore the warning signs and the messengers who are trying to get you back into balance? Do you think of your body as something you must love?

Nora, a biochemistry researcher, found that changing how she looked at her body changed her life. For years, Nora had struggled with all kinds of diets and regimes without any success. When she had a serious health scare, she told herself that this was the last straw. She had to get into shape. It was now or never.

Fast forward three months. That's when I met a new Nora, with a triumphant smile on her face. She had astounded herself and her friends by losing more weight than she had ever thought possible in so short a time. "I tend to be in my head a lot," she admitted, "and so I never took much time to pay attention to my body. Once I started doing what was good for me physically, I saw that it wasn't about losing the weight but about *loving my body*. That made all the difference. Being careful about what I feed myself isn't hard when I think about it like that."

You don't have to be overweight to identify with Nora. With the hectic pace of our lives, when something has to give it's often our bodies that get the short end of the stick, whether that's reflected in the meals we skip, the fast foods we gobble down on the run, the excessive stimulants we drink, or the exercise we never quite fit in. The problem is that when we don't keep our body in balance, the rest of us—our mind, our emotions, our spirit, our relationships—suffer as well.

There is a scene in the book *Zorba the Greek* that sums up the importance of caring for our bodies. The earthy Zorba never does anything without total resilience and passion. Zorba's boss has yet to learn the joys of this life-affirming lifestyle. When his boss, head buried in a book and in the clouds, claims he's not hungry and doesn't want to eat the delicious meal Zorba has just prepared, Zorba exclaims, "But you've not had a bite since morning. The body's got a soul, too, have pity on it. Give it something to eat, boss, give it something; it's our beast of burden, you know. If you don't feed it, it'll leave you stranded in the middle o' the road."[1]

THE ILLUSION OF BEING FULL

Another myth that makes it hard to give ourselves the attention we deserve is the myth that busyness is strength—that the more balls we can juggle, the stronger we are. When we seem to have the ability to keep pushing—to go, go, go—we believe that we can do anything. We think that we're members of that special breed who are built to give and who don't need to rest and take breaks as much as everyone else. This is, in fact, a trick we play on ourselves. The truth is that often the more driven we are, the less energy we really have.

Brendan Kelly, an acupuncturist and herbalist who specializes in Chinese five-element acupuncture, talked to me about how this works, because, admittedly, I'm one of those who has managed to fool myself. Like all healing traditions, there are many ways of looking at how energy works in the body and in our lives, and what follows is just one interpretation of the classic Chinese view of how the body, mind, and spirit work together. It's based on the idea that the body naturally needs alternating cycles of activity and rest so that we can replenish our reservoir of strength.

An abundance of activity in our lives creates what Chinese medicine looks at as "heat" in the body. The heat we produce by our constant busyness uses up our body's "coolant," which we need in order to maintain our internal resources and reserves. When we use too much of our reserves and have much more heat than coolant, we can start to have a variety of symptoms, anything from anxiety and insomnia to hot flashes, redness, or heat anywhere in the body. "This coolant is what the Chinese call yin energy, and it is one source, though not the exclusive source, for our internal peace as well as deep wisdom," Brendan explained. "What happens when we burn out this coolant is that we are sacrificing the possibility of deep peace and wisdom for short-term activity and busyness."

In other words, by keeping our lives full of activity without taking time to reenergize, we create "a lack of internal peace and we don't have the ability to listen to who we are," said Brendan. "Without enough 'coolant,' we cannot know who we are in our heart or express who we are in a balanced way." As you might expect, we can rebuild our yin energy (our coolant) by relaxing and creating a state of stillness, whether by giving ourselves more breaks or more sleep, engaging in prayer or meditation, or using certain healing therapies.

Now, here's how we trick ourselves. The less strength or resources we have within, the more we may sense an internal inadequacy, as if we just don't have enough to keep going. None of us likes that feeling, so we tend to push even harder to make up for it. We pump ourselves up with stimulants, fill our days with activity, and create more external busyness. All of that masks the feeling that we're really running on empty. The busyness, the activity, and the stimulants conceal our internal depletion and create the illusion that we have more energy than we do. Our modern, fast-paced culture adds to the illusion by encouraging the buzz of busyness. We are skilled at creating all sorts of products and elixirs to help us keep on buzzing. But all along, the internal buzz that we label as energy isn't real energy. Instead, it indicates a lack of real energy.

"The extra heat in the body gives us the impression that we have more energy," says Brendan, "but we don't have more energy—just more heat. When you use heat instead of real energy to propel you through the day, what you give up is a sense of internal well-being." What's the difference between that and a state where we are truly energized and full? When we have ample inner resources, we don't rush to and fro. Instead, we are at peace and have inner stability because we feel full and secure. We take care of what needs to be done, but we aren't consumed by the compulsive need to push beyond what our bodies can handle at the moment because we know that we cannot continue to give to others if we ourselves aren't full.

MYTH:
My drive to stay busy and my ability
to keep doing more means I am strong.

MAGIC:
Stillness creates strength.

A classic image that is sometimes used as an analogy for this process is that of a fire (heat) burning beneath a bowl (our body) that is holding water (our yin coolant). The fire heats the water and creates steam, which represents what the Chinese call ch'i, our vital energy or essential life force. The ch'i is the sustaining energy we need to live. When things are in balance, the fire creates a natural warming effect. But if the fire becomes too hot, the water begins to boil. If this goes on too long, the heat literally consumes the water and dissipates the energy we need to bank our inner fire. Once the water is boiled away, we can literally collapse because we are not able to produce any more energy, or ch'i. "When this happens, the results can be dramatic," says Brendan. "One month you feel that you have a lot of energy and the next month you fall off the cliff—you're in bed and you can't move."

Are you running on a full tank or are you running on the illusion of a full tank? Do you let your tank become empty before you fill it up again and therefore run the risk of stalling out? Do you let your light go out because you don't have enough oil in your inner lamp? In short, where do you put yourself on the list of priorities in your life? Too often we relegate our needs to the bottom of the list, if we're on the list at all. We take care of our duties and obligations to others first and use the energy that's left over for ourselves. But, truthfully, how often is there any energy left over?

What if we reversed that order? What if we made sure our lamp had enough oil in it first before lighting the way for others? Wouldn't that help us keep our lamp burning strong so we could give more light to others? To do that, we must learn to recognize our inner needs and then draw healthy boundaries so we have the time and energy to fill those needs. To renew ourselves so that we can continue to give, and give well, we must embrace the paradox that *saying no will enable us to say yes.*

If the idea of saying no makes you cringe, know that this principle comes straight out of spiritual tradition. The greatest teachers knew how to say no. Like all of us, they needed time alone to recharge and renew. Even an indefatigable missionary of mercy like Mother Teresa taught that renewal is a prerequisite for strength. She said that renewal is what gives us the energy to continue serving others. She observed that "the contemplatives and ascetics of all ages and religions have sought God in the silence and solitude of the desert, forest, and mountain" and said that we, too, are called to withdraw at certain intervals.[2] It is when we are alone with God in silence, she said, that "we accumulate the inward power which we distribute in action."[3]

She was following the advice of her own teacher. Jesus did the same after he fed the multitudes the loaves and fishes. He told his disciples to go into the boat ahead of him, and "when he had sent the multitudes away, he went up into a mountain apart to pray: and when the evening was come, he was there alone." With a somewhat lighter touch on the same topic, John Barrymore once joked that "God said it is not good for man to be alone, but sometimes it is a great relief!"

During the natural ebb and flow of our week, we all need relief. That's when drawing boundaries (saying no politely, of course) is appropriate, something you'll explore further in the next chapter. When your energy is ebbing, it's time to shift gears from an active orientation of giving energy to a receptive one of receiving. It's time to plug back in to your energy source and do what most reenergizes you—whether it's walking in nature, listening to a favorite piece of music, playing a game, or simply closing your eyes, doing nothing, and taking a long, deep breath.

GETTING TO KNOW YOU

Instead of pushing yourself beyond your limits and pumping yourself up with more stimulants so that you can fulfill more commitments to others, honoring yourself calls for a different habit. It asks you to become conscious of what *you* need, right now, inside and out. In order for you to put down this book and do what you must to regain balance, and to remember to do it tomorrow and the next day and the next, you first have to know yourself.

"*I know myself*"—it's one of the most profound statements we can ever make. Self-knowledge, after all, is the ultimate goal extolled by mystics and masters the world around. Inscribed in the forecourt of Apollo's temple at Delphi was the famous command "Know thyself." The Book of Thomas the Contender says, "He who has not known himself has known nothing,"[4] and the Zohar, from the Jewish mystical tradition of the Kabbalah, encourages, "Go to your self, know your self, fulfill your self."[5]

One of the reasons you may not take specific actions to fill your own needs is simply that you don't really know yourself at the most basic level. You don't know how you really feel and what you really need. While "knowing yourself" is a lifelong goal that has deeper and deeper layers of meaning, you can take tiny steps toward that goal every day. Here's a simple question that can help you refocus on what you need to do to come back into balance: *What do I need right now to be happy?*

When I've asked myself that question, I often answer that to do my most creative work, I need quiet and I need regular doses of fresh air out in nature. Yet awareness alone is not enough. If I don't care enough to honor myself, to put those needs on my priority list, I won't remember to turn to those antidotes when I begin to feel cranky or anxious. When things start spinning out of control, unless I make a point of asking myself that question again and again, I forget to fill my lungs with fresh air. I forget to take control and create the quiet I need by turning off the phones, refusing to look at my e-mail, or physically moving myself to a quiet spot to work.

A friend who works out of her home reminded me of how empowering it can be to know yourself and then act on that knowing. One day I asked her when was the best time for us to meet. She immediately replied in a straightforward way, "It's better for me to meet in the late afternoon. If I go out in the morning, I'm tempted to start doing errands. I stop here and there on my way back to my office, and I just don't get the work done that I need to do." She knew that much about herself and therefore she could set up a schedule that was best for her. Like many of the methods for honoring yourself, this doesn't sound difficult, but it takes practice. The change starts with watching yourself, getting to know yourself, and then translating that knowledge into action that honors your needs.

KEYS TO THE
BALANCING ACT

Watch for the Warning Signs

The first step to bringing your life back into balance is to be able to recognize when you are out of balance. What are the warning signs that consistently appear in your life to tell you that your life is becoming lopsided? Here are a few warning signs that can help you become more aware of the messengers who have entered your life to let you know where you need to make adjustments.

■ **Prolonged tension or anxiety.** Tension is not bad. It's what impels us to act and what creates breakthroughs. Prolonged tension, however, especially when we feel it in our bodies, can be a signal that we have extended ourselves too far—that we aren't paying attention to our inner needs and are letting our reserves dwindle. Some of us are used to putting ourselves second or third or last, and we have been conditioned to ignore the signals. You can change that habit by noticing when you feel tense or anxious. When you feel *a tension*, pay *attention*. Awareness is the first step back to honoring yourself.

■ **Lack of focus.** Your mind and emotions will play tricks on you when you don't meet your own needs. I've found that if I don't take enough time to play or have fun, I sabotage myself. I can't sit still, I'm distracted, and I procrastinate. I've made a decision to deny myself a few moments of playfulness so I can concentrate on the task at hand, but in reality I've done just the opposite. I've made focusing impossible because my needs aren't being met. As a result, I find all sorts of excuses not to settle down (the garden needs weeding, the dishes need to be put away, the cats need a massage), and then I criticize myself for my lack of focus. Be sure to regularly refresh and renew so you aren't subconsciously sabotaging yourself.

■ **Griping.** Complaining and nagging can actually be a way of communicating. They are often just a code for "I have unmet needs and you're not taking notice." They are another way of saying, "I don't want to give you the impression that I'm needy, but since you are not picking up my unspoken signals, I'll have to convey my unhappiness in other ways." We complain about the clothes on the floor or the dishes in the sink when we are really trying to say that we need help, support, or a break. If you hear yourself or others griping, it's time to gently ask what's really making you (or them) unhappy and then to listen closely for the answers.

■ **Physical and emotional symptoms.** Your body and your emotions can react in a range of ways when you aren't giving yourself the attention you need. Watch for the reactions that are unique to you. Is it tight shoulders, frequent sighing, headaches, a knot in your stomach, sleeplessness, tears, outbursts of anger, overeating, or undereating? Remember that these responses are not bad in and of themselves. They serve a function. They are speaking to you. Your job is to find out what they are saying. The real story is always underneath the symptoms. Practice looking for what's underneath.

Seven Steps for Staying in Balance

Martha Graham, the celebrated twentieth-century American dancer and choreographer, once said, "I believe that we learn by practice. Whether it means to learn to dance by practicing dancing or to learn to live by practicing living, the principles are the same." Here are seven ways to put what you are learning about yourself into action so you can practice honoring yourself in big ways and small. You can also use the following statements, as well as all the "magic" statements that are set off throughout this book, as affirmations. Say them silently or aloud to remind yourself to focus on moving beyond the myths to the magic of honoring yourself.

❶ I get in touch with how I feel. You may not be stating your needs or taking steps to meet them simply because you aren't in touch with how you feel and what you want and need. Practice asking yourself throughout the day: *How do I feel right now? What do I need most right now? What will make me feel more joyful and at peace?* It's the small things that make the most difference when you do them each day. Every action you take to honor yourself also sends a signal to others about what you think you deserve and therefore how you expect to be treated.

❷ I eliminate either/or thinking. Catch yourself when you are sinking into either/or thinking that tries to cut you out of the picture. You may hear yourself saying things like "I have to take care of this situation immediately, so I don't have time for myself right now. I have to choose between him and me, and I can't abandon him." Unfortunately, when we fall into thinking "it's either this *or* that," it's usually our own needs that fall by the wayside. If you feel the either/or tug of war coming on, tell yourself: *I have a right and a duty to give to myself. When I am in need, I must also receive.*

❸ I take preventative measures. Take action before you get caught in a lopsided approach to giving and receiving. For instance, if you know you have a tendency to develop a headache, backache, or shoulder ache once a week, be proactive in caring for yourself. Make sure you get away from your desk and stretch, take a break, exercise, or schedule a regular massage. Take time to check in with yourself regularly. Schedule that reminder on your daily planner so you won't forget.

❹ I check in with my whole self. We have needs on all four levels of our life—physical, emotional, mental, and spiritual. So when you're checking in with yourself, assess each of those areas and ask, "Which part of me needs attention right now?" If you are feeling emotionally fragile, you may need to get support by talking to a friend. If you're tired, you may need more rest or exercise. If you're mentally bored, seek out stimulation and challenge, maybe by attending a new event, cultivating a hobby, or signing up for a class. If you're feeling a spiritual void and are missing meaning in your life, do something that helps you get back in touch with your spirit. Figure out what part of you needs energizing and commit to nurturing it back to health.

❺ I celebrate my victories. If you have accomplished a certain amount of work or met a goal, even a small one, reward yourself by doing something fun and rejuvenating. Even little rewards—watching a favorite movie, buying yourself some flowers, attending a play or musical event—will help you value yourself. It will also train you to give back to yourself and replenish your inner reservoir of strength.

6 I take simple steps. If it's difficult for you to let yourself receive, start with baby steps. At a time in my life when my finances were tight, those baby steps helped me climb out of my rut. In those days, I was very stingy with myself, only allowing myself to buy absolute necessities. The world around me seemed to reflect my rigid ways. When I began to let myself buy something as simple as a yummy snack or a new piece of clothing, things seemed to change and more money starting flowing into my life. What was really changing was my own attitude. By depriving myself, I had, in essence, been affirming that this was how I wanted to be treated and the kind of world I expected to live in. By giving to myself, I was changing what I wanted that world to look like. What small step can you consistently take that looks like the kind of world you want to live in?

7 I accept compliments. Do you have a habit of telling people who compliment you, "Oh, it was nothing," or of saying to someone who unexpectedly gives you a gift, "Oh, you didn't have to do that." If you can't receive compliments or gifts from others, you are communicating—to them and to yourself—that you don't think you are worthy of receiving. And if you can't easily accept those compliments or gifts, how are you going to react to the abundance, gifts, and great relationships the universe wants to bring you? Will you say, "Oh, you didn't have to do that"? Or will you say, "Thank you! I'm grateful, I appreciate it, and I'm open to more!"

CHAPTER 3

SETTING BOUNDARIES

To try to benefit others, and yet not to have enough
of oneself to give others, is a poor affair.
— RABINDRANATH TAGORE

"I have a question," said the young woman in the medi tation circle as she brushed aside a stray piece of hair that had fallen across her face. She shot a glance at her boyfriend, seated beside her, and he nodded, encouraging her to go on. "It has to do with termites," she said.

My husband and I were traveling in northern California and had joined this weekly meditation group for the evening at the invitation of his uncle. That night about a dozen people, young and old, singles and couples, from different walks of life, were sitting in a circle along with the long-time meditation teacher. After the meditation, each member of the group had the opportunity to talk.

"We're facing a crisis," the young woman continued as everyone listened intently. "We understand the idea of having compassion for all life and trying not to harm others. But we found out that our house is infested with termites and we don't know what to do. It doesn't seem right to kill them."

The meditation teacher, John, was quiet for a moment and then asked, "What will happen if you let the termites stay?"

"They'll destroy the whole structure of the house," replied the girl's boyfriend, who was as distraught as she was. "The house will fall apart. We won't be able to live there any longer and, of course, no one will want to buy the house. I suppose the termites could go on to destroy other houses in the neighborhood too."

John explained to the group that the ideal of harmlessness asks us to protect life and not to injure living beings, but it does not demand that we abandon common sense or practicality. Then he did what good teachers do best. He asked questions. "If someone was trying to rape your wife, maim your husband, or kidnap your child, would you let them?" he asked. "If a murderer enters your home and you do not take action to stop him, are you protecting the life of your family—are you espousing harmlessness then? If an insect is carrying a disease that will kill many people, would it be right to kill the disease-carriers in order to protect the community? If termites destroy your home, whose life are you sacrificing and whose life are you saving? Each of us must answer these questions for ourselves."

While deciding whether or not to get rid of termites may seem like an extreme example, in fact it's parallel to many challenges we face. Have you ever asked yourself questions like these: How far should I let this situation go before I draw the line? Am I doing the right thing by sacrificing myself or am I jeopardizing what's most important to me? By giving so much of myself to support this person, am I actually holding him back—and holding myself back too? Susan, once a neighbor of mine, discovered that her son's happiness and her own depended on the answer to that last question.

REINVESTING IN YOURSELF

As a single mom, sacrifice was Susan's middle name. She believed that giving was the gateway to goodness—that if she gave enough, everything would work out just fine. Her son, Jake, had always been shy and had difficulty relating to others, a trait that didn't change even when he was in his early twenties. He didn't want to leave the house, couldn't hold down a job, and at times would have what amounted to a violent tantrum.

Susan was becoming more and more worried about him and thought it might help if she arranged to work from home, where she could keep an eye on what was really going on and give him extra support. Despite her many sacrifices, Jake didn't improve and she finally sought professional help. Susan realized that they had to take some bold steps. She suggested to Jake that he try living in a group home within traveling distance from her. Reluctantly, he agreed. That single act of separation turned out to be a catalyst for transformation, for mother and son. Within months, both of their lives took an upward turn.

"I had become his crutch," Susan later admitted to me when she saw how much progress her son was making in the right environment. Keeping our children as comfortable as they can be is not always the answer, she said. There was a time when giving unconditional support to Jake was the right thing to do, but that time wasn't forever. Now she was learning the lesson that *in order to give her son more, she needed to give him less*. She was learning to embrace paradox.

The new boundaries also freed Susan to take a look at her own life. She saw that by carrying around the false belief that "sacrifice is the answer to everything," she had also been putting her own life on hold. Now that she had more time to pay attention to herself, she realized that she wasn't really happy in her career. She didn't even like where she was living and desperately needed new vistas herself. When she felt sure that Jake was secure in his new surroundings, she started searching for a new place to live. Five months later, she was ready to move. When I said goodbye to Susan, she was full of energy and looked the happiest I had ever seen her.

MYTH:
*I support those I love most
by sacrificing for them.*

MAGIC:
*To give more,
I must sometimes give less.*

In an interview with Forbes.com, legendary management guru Peter Drucker, at the age of 95, talked about boundaries and said that a key issue for leaders is to learn how to say no. "Don't tell me what you're doing," he said. "Tell me what you *stopped* doing." Leaders who always say yes are very popular, he added, but they get nothing done. Drucker advised leaders not to have more than two priorities at a time and he spoke about the importance of delegating what we're not good at doing. "Never try to be an expert if you are not," he said. "Build on your strengths and find strong people to do the other necessary tasks."[1]

We are all leaders—if not at work, then in our communities, in our families, or in the most important domain: the domain of self. You are, literally, leading your own life. Whether in business or in daily life, you choose how to use the resources you have been given; and the most valuable of those resources are your time, energy, and attention. What you choose to do or not to do with them will determine whether or not you will thrive or barely survive.

Like those running a successful business, you also need to reinvest the right amount of resources back into yourself. In addition to helping and giving to others, do you nurture and sustain the inner powerhouse that makes the whole operation of your life hum? Or do you become depleted and burned out because you are spread too thin? If you're trying to do too much at once, you may suffocate yourself, which is how Drucker described those who succumb to the mindset that saying yes to everything is best. Healthy boundaries are not optional; they are critical.

CAN GIVING BE DANGEROUS TO YOUR HEALTH?

Drawing healthy boundaries is more than a cute turn of phrase. Proper boundaries that lead to self-care can actually keep us healthy. More and more scientific research is showing, for example, that chronic stress, a symptom of imbalance in the flow of giving and receiving, has a direct link to our health. One study indicated that women who were experiencing chronic stress or who perceived that they were undergoing high stress had telomeres inside their immune cells that had undergone significant aging (telomeres are the sections of DNA at the tips of our chromosomes). Dennis Novack of Drexel University College of Medicine said that this important study "demonstrated that there is no such thing as a separation of mind and body—the very molecules in our bodies are responsive to our psychological environment."[2] Other studies have linked stress, helplessness, hopelessness, and suppressed emotions to the onset or progression of cancer. When we don't draw necessary boundaries and learn how to replenish ourselves, when we suppress rather than express our needs, we can jeopardize our lives.

So, can giving be dangerous to your health? If it keeps you from acknowledging and expressing your valid needs, yes. If it detracts from your ability to continue giving joyfully and abundantly to others, yes. If your giving stunts another's growth or your own, yes, it can be dangerous.

The habit of giving too much to others and not enough to ourselves can also sabotage our most essential task in life—walking our own path of self-discovery. In *The Hero Within*, Carol Pearson points out that because the role of women has traditionally been tied to nurturing and fulfilling their duties, women will often "forbear taking their journey because they fear it will hurt their husbands, fathers, mothers, children, or friends."[3] (Taking our "journeys" in this sense does not, of course, refer to a physical journey but to pursuing our own internal quest to discover what we can uniquely contribute within our circle of influence.) Likewise, says Pearson, men may refuse to take their journeys when they believe that their fragile wives need protection. The idea that such sacrifices are helping our loved ones is an illusion. By sacrificing our personal journeys or by allowing others to oppress us, we are not helping but hurting them.

By reinforcing someone's dependent behavior, we actually indulge their less-developed self, Pearson explains. For that reason, she says, "one of the worst things a woman can do for a man's soul is to allow him to oppress her." Similarly, whenever a man holds himself back because he thinks his partner is inept, he "reinforces in her that attitude about herself and hence helps cripple her," when in reality "her stronger, wiser self wants to grow and wants him to grow too."[4]

Underneath the myth that sacrifice is always right, then, lies the subtle misconception that if we do not automatically drop everything to sacrifice for others, we are abandoning them in their time of need. Yet, as we've seen, the opposite can be true. Sacrificing for others can hold them back, and it can hold us back.

MYTH:
When others are in need, I must sacrifice for them.
Sacrifice is always the right thing to do.

MAGIC:
Sacrifice can stunt those I think I am helping.
When I am true to myself, I help others
be true to themselves.

Depending on the circumstances and the timing, giving can be nurturing or toxic, compassionate or crippling. We can get beyond the myth that sacrifice is always right to the magic of balance by learning to live in harmony with this powerful principle: *When we are true to ourselves, we help others be true to themselves. When we draw the boundaries that enable us to grow, we help others grow too.*

HIDING BEHIND SACRIFICE

In an odd sort of way, at subconscious levels we may actually welcome extreme self-sacrifice because it secretly provides us with an excuse. Sacrificing for others is an excuse for not having to take responsibility for our lives. It's a way to avoid the confrontations that may come when we begin to honor ourselves and assert our right to be at the top of our priority list.

Or we may be addicted to sacrifice because we don't feel worthy inside and it feels good when someone else desperately needs us.

Ultimately, all that comes with a cost. Sacrifice can be a mask that we put on and then become so used to that we forget that the face we are showing to the world, and to ourselves, is not our real face. Just as we can hide our internal depletion behind more and more external busyness, so we can hide our true selves behind a mountain of sacrifice.

Sacrifice is a beautiful virtue when it comes from the heart. But to use sacrifice as a way to avoid facing our fears or shaping our own futures, is a cop-out. It's handing over our choices to someone else, when the cornerstone of honoring ourselves is making our own choices. It's like taking a long, bumpy ride in the back seat of someone else's car (and typically it's not a limo) when you should be in the driver's seat, or like accepting a supporting role in someone else's drama when you should be playing the leading role in your own life story.

At times, sacrifice looks like the easy way out. It may seem convenient for someone else to call all the shots. That way we can say, "It's not my fault," when things don't seem to be going right. We've all been tempted to blame others for events in our lives. Don't feel ashamed when you notice the blame. Instead, use it to grow. Recognize it as a messenger who has come to wake you up.

When you find yourself blaming anyone for anything, you can be sure you have been duped by the subtle and insidious myth that the determining factors in your life are outside of yourself—that someone else is responsible to fill you up or to fix what's making you unhappy. Nothing could be farther from the truth.

As long as you believe that it is not your job to bring the scales of your life back into balance, you will continue to accept less than the best for yourself as you passively wait for someone to rescue you. It's not someone else's job to fill you up, and you don't need anyone's permission to do that job yourself. Only you can know when it's time to take a break, put on your favorite music, go away for the weekend, or leave a job or relationship because it's no longer right for you. When we blame others, we take on the role of helpless victim and we abdicate one of the most important rights and powers we have: freedom of choice. No matter what circumstances you are in, no matter what has gone before, you always have the power to make a new choice— starting now.

MYTH:
Someone else is responsible to fill me up
and to fix what's making me unhappy.

MAGIC:
I am responsible for how my life unfolds. The choice for
what happens next in my life is always my own.

The next time you find yourself asking in your head or aloud, "How could they do this to me? What's wrong with them? How can I get them to change so I can get what I need?" turn the myth into magic. Say to yourself instead: "My choices, my attitudes, and my actions will determine what happens next in my life. I have the power to make a new and higher choice. My happiness is not based on what they do but on what I do." Grandma Moses, the twentieth-century American folk artist who started painting in her seventies and lived until she was

101, was a testament to the power of choice. "If I didn't start painting, I would have raised chickens," she said. "Life is what we make it, always has been, always will be."

SACRIFICE AS SELFISHNESS

There is yet another reason we may choose to hide behind a habit of sacrifice, even though we grumble about all the "duties" we're saddled with. We may purposely spend all our time giving to others so that there won't be any time left over for our primary duty—being all we can be. *I WANT YOUR Best & MINE TOO*

Why would we want to sidestep this soul journey? Sometimes we are afraid that if we get in touch with our real passion in life, the conditions we have become accustomed to will change dramatically. We may have to move, give up a relationship, or take the risk of starting a new career. We may fear that we're not good enough or that we might be rejected if we embrace our highest calling. These fears are all natural, and I talk about them more in Part Four, "Celebrating Yourself and Honoring Your Own Voice." But know that they are just fears—they are not you.

It is in the realm of sacrifice, then, that we meet yet another paradox: *Sacrifice can be a way to give your best self* and *sacrifice can be a way to hide your best self.* Put another way, *sacrifice can be the epitome of selfishness.*

We all come into life with special qualities and gifts that we are meant to develop and share with others. When you hide behind some perceived duty as an excuse for not having the time to develop your talents and give your own gifts, that so-called sacrifice is, in reality, selfishness because you are withholding the gifts you were born to give. By postponing your adventure, you are shortchanging those who are waiting to receive your gifts. The best thing any of us can do for the world is not to hide behind sacrifice but to make the real sacrifice of stepping into the highest role we can fill in this moment.

Examining why you find it difficult to draw proper boundaries is not necessarily an easy or a comfortable task, but it's a worthwhile one. We cannot truly heal unless we deal with the underlying issues at the core of our symptoms. To discover why you may be giving so much to others without giving to yourself, consider starting with this truth: When we avoid doing anything, it's usually because we fear what it will bring. What do you fear will happen if you draw boundaries or if you don't sacrifice? Are you afraid that saying no will make others unhappy, and do you believe that it's your job to make them happy? Are you afraid that if you don't do what other people want you to do, they will reject you? Do you believe that you have to be compliant in order to be loved?

[handwritten margin note: Look under the surface for the true reason]

There are good reasons, of course, why we have developed such beliefs. Perhaps as children we learned to please others to avoid the pain of disapproval, the sting of criticism, or even the threat of aggression. Perhaps we were raised in families or cultures where that kind of behavior was expected or praised. Nevertheless, to continue to follow this pattern without question, even though we have a gnawing feeling inside that something is amiss, is a slow form of suicide.

Don't be afraid to engage in some deep soul-searching to understand what is driving you to consistently put others first. Once you acknowledge why you may be addicted to sacrifice, you can begin to counter the myths and retrain yourself to react differently. You'll become better at catching yourself before a situation gets too far out of hand. Tell yourself that it's okay to be loyal to yourself first for a change. You have a right to hold your own opinions, defend your rights, and make your own decisions. You can choose to be around people who are supportive rather than domineering. You deserve companions who are interested in what you have to say and don't feel the need to suppress you. You can honor yourself.

CHECKS AND BALANCES

Mastering the balancing act of giving and receiving takes a change in perspective. Giving and receiving, setting boundaries and tearing them down, honoring ourselves and honoring others—these are not opposites but complements. The more we see them that way, the more adept we become at sensing when it's time to draw boundaries and when it's time to step out of them.

The Jewish mystical tradition of Kabbalah says that dancing with the paradox of giving and receiving is a natural part of life's creative tension. This paradox is embodied in Kabbalah's Tree of Life, a kind of blueprint of reality, of how our world was created, and of how it works. The Tree of Life is made up of ten "sefirot," which represent the archetypal forces or qualities that exist in the divine world and in everything, including us. Some of these forces work as complementary pairs of opposites, a system of checks and balances. Each pair needs to be in dynamic tension to ensure that neither one gets out of hand. One of those pairs is Hesed and Gevurah. They have much to teach us about boundaries and balance.

Hesed is the force of loving-kindness, mercy, and expansion. We tend to think of love, mercy, and openness as positive qualities, and they are. The sages of Kabbalah noted, however, that even loving-kindness, when taken to the extreme, can get out of balance. Without some kind of form or vessel to hold and give them shape, the generous qualities of mercy and love, like an unbridled waterfall, cannot be contained and harnessed for good. Have you ever known people who are "expansive"—they have lots of ideas and energy—but they never seem to be able to accomplish anything? That's because without discipline and structure, they cannot focus and give form to their brilliance.

Since the expansive qualities of generosity and openness can go off the deep end, we need to set limits and give definition to our giving. We need Gevurah. Gevurah is the force that represents justice, judgment, and power in the world and within us. It provides structure and boundaries as well as discipline and discrimination.

Yet, just as the energy of expansion needs limits and boundaries, so the opposite is true. Too many boundaries and too much structure send us to the other extreme. Rigid structures and mindsets that subscribe to the letter and never the spirit of the law clamp shut the open hand and heart of our creativity. An overemphasis on structure and rules may, in fact, rule out the very thing we most need in order to stay in balance. In what may be more familiar terms, Shakespeare speaks of the need to balance boundaries with openness, and generosity with restraint, in *The Merchant of Venice*, where Portia so eloquently counsels: "Earthly power doth then show likest God's when mercy seasons justice."

RESOLUTION THROUGH THE HEART

How do we reconcile the complementary forces of mercy and judgment, of openness and structure that sometimes wage war within us and around us? Like other wisdom teachings, Kabbalah teaches that resolution comes through the heart. In Kabbalah, the heart corresponds to another archetypal force, Tiferet. Tiferet means "Beauty" and it represents the great integrator and harmonizer.

The world's traditions are filled with poignant lessons that point to the wisdom of the heart. We learn from the sages that the voice of the heart will always tell us the right way to go in any situation. In the ancient Brihadaranyaka Upanishad, when the sage Yajnavalkya is asked, "Where is the locality of truth?" he answers, "In the heart, for by the heart man knows truth." When you are attuned to your heart, you will know when it is appropriate to preserve boundaries for the good of all involved and when you would be better off throwing those boundaries out the window.

This tale from the Hasidic tradition of Judaism shows that rigidly following rules and expectations can close down our capacity to give from the heart. Every week a respected rabbi celebrated a weekly Sabbath meal with friends and students. One week, a new guest showed up. As the meal got underway, those attending looked with disdain on the newcomer, who was sloppily dressed and a bit crude. On top of it, seemingly without respect for the rabbi, the man pulled a large radish out of his pocket and gnawed away at it loudly. The rabbi, however, seemed not to notice. One of the rabbi's students, unable to stand it any longer, turned to the man and was about to reprimand him when the rabbi interrupted and said, "You know, I wish I had a nice big radish to eat with this wonderful meal." Hearing the teacher's words, the new guest reached into his pocket, pulled out another radish, and handed it to his host, who gave him a big smile and thanked him for his kindness. Simple stories like this are full of symbology. They tell us that when we catch ourselves judging our own or another's behavior, we might just need to let those walls we've erected come crashing down so we can bask in the light of the heart.

We all have to deal with situations that get way off center and out of control. When that happens, we honor ourselves and others by coming back to center, to our center. For creative problem-solving comes from the heart. Not only that, but the more we come back to our heart center, the more we magnetize other players in the scenario back to center as well. Even if someone involved in the situation remains stuck in their position, when you stay in the center you will be able to see more clearly what to do.

Alan Watts, a key interpreter of Eastern philosophies for the West in the twentieth century, once explained this point when he was talking about Zen meditation as an analogy for life. He said that it's wise to "live from your center" for the same reason that we are taught to stay in the center in the martial arts. "If you expect something to come in a certain way, you position yourself to get ready for it," he said. "If it comes another way, by the time you reposition your energy, it is too late. So stay in the center, and you will be ready to move in any direction."[5]

When I had a job supervising a large department that needed lots of hands-on attention, I saw that sometimes a little adjustment back to center could go a long way. Although I was asked to manage this team, I was also responsible for producing a major portion of the work. My intense schedule and responsibilities made it difficult to give as much attention to my co-workers as I would have liked and, as a result, things didn't always work smoothly. The squabbles that started appearing weekly only took up more of my time and made the pressure worse. With the restraints of my schedule (my boundaries) and my preconceived notion that I didn't have time to be a good manager (my mental mindset), it was no wonder there were problems. I had to find my way back toward center.

At first I felt like the victim, but that point of view wasn't solving the problem. I realized that I had to focus on what I could do to improve the situation instead of wishing that others would magically change overnight. So I tried to see the situation from the perspective of my heart and I asked myself: What choices can I make to transform this situation?

I started by taking a good look at my office. The first thing anyone saw as they entered was the cold shoulder of a filing cabinet and me hiding behind my computer screen. Neither was inviting or friendly. I rearranged my office so that when people entered they could clearly see me. I made room for a chair on the other side of my desk, where my co-workers could sit and feel more welcome. Second, I recognized that a few talented people in particular needed attention more than others. I created a reminder on my calendar to check in with them at least once a week to make sure we could work out issues before they became time bombs. By tearing down some boundaries, I moved a little more toward center and so did those I worked with.

KEYS TO THE
BALANCING ACT

Take the Litmus Test

Bill Cosby once said, "I don't know the key to success, but the key to failure is trying to please everybody." There are times when sacrifice is called for, and there are times when, in the extreme, sacrifice can harm you and others. Do you balance sacrificing for others with drawing boundaries so you can focus on what's important to you and reinvest in yourself? This litmus test will help you find out where you may need to make adjustments.

■ Do I automatically say yes whenever anyone asks for my help or needs a problem solved? Or do I politely but firmly set boundaries when I need to?

■ Do I always put myself at the bottom of my to-do list? Or do I regularly ask myself what I want and need and then schedule that action into my day as a priority?

■ Do I allow people or events to pull me away from what I plan to do? Or am I literally leading my own life by setting my direction and acting on the values and goals that matter to me?

■ Do I let friends or loved ones consistently monopolize conversations or bully me into going along with their decisions? Or do I speak up, clearly express how I feel, and stand up for myself?

(handwritten in left margin: what is your purpose?)

■ Would I rather please others than have a confrontation with them? Or do I challenge invasive and inappropriate behavior and correct others' misperceptions, even if it means they may not like what I have to say?

■ Does my giving to others prevent them from doing their share or from moving forward on their life's journey? Or do I draw boundaries so that others do not become overly dependent on me to their detriment?

■ Do I hide behind my sacrifices, filling my time doing things for others to avoid embracing my own calling? Or do I put a priority on developing my talents so I can give my gifts to others?

Seven Steps to Setting Healthy Boundaries

Honoring yourself by drawing healthy boundaries is not about leaving others out but about counting yourself in. As the Hasidic master Rabbi Moshe Leib once said, "A human being who does not have a single hour of his own every day is no human being at all." If you've answered the preceding questions, you have a clearer idea of where you may need to draw better boundaries to honor your own needs. All of us get off balance from time to time. What matters is not that it happens but that we become better at recognizing when it is happening so we can quickly take steps to restore balance. Here are seven ways you can begin to set healthy boundaries.

❶ **Practice on the small things.** When you are not used to drawing boundaries, it can feel uncomfortable at first to do so. Practice on a small, everyday issue, like turning off your phone when you need to concentrate rather than being at everyone's beck and call, asking a family member to make dinner or do an errand, or telling friends you're not available on an evening when you want to spend time alone. As you learn to set boundaries in situations like these, you'll find it easier to recognize and confront the larger issues when they surface.

Me ❷ **Clearly communicate your needs.** Most people aren't mind readers. They won't know what you need unless you tell them. Be specific when expressing your needs. State your feelings and requests lovingly but firmly, couching them in terms of your needs and not what you think the other person is doing wrong. Drawing a boundary does not mean you have to make someone else wrong. It's about stating what you need and deserve.

Still does not guarantee you will get what you want or they will respect accordingly.

Them ❸ **Exercise your freedom of choice.** When someone asks you to do something, rather than automatically saying yes, practice asking yourself: *What are my choices? What do I want and what do I feel is right for me in this situation? Is sacrificing in this case appropriate? What's most important to me right now?*

❹ **Put yourself at the top of your priority list.** Don't wait until you've checked off the tasks you are doing for others to give yourself what you need. Schedule time for yourself so that your own self-care isn't the item that gets constantly bumped off your list of priorities. Recharging your inner batteries is not optional. It's a bona fide part of your schedule.

❺ **Narrow your focus.** Good leaders don't just decide what they are going to do; they identify what they are *not* going to do. As the leader of your own life, what can you do to become more focused? What can you delegate, hire someone else to do, or cut altogether from your to-do list to ensure that you are investing your precious time and energy in the best place? By focusing your resources where you can make the greatest impact, you'll have more to give where it counts.

⑥ Problem solve from the heart. The sages teach that a quiet heart can lead us to the best solutions to any problem. When you are facing a knotty issue involving boundaries, look at it from a heart perspective. Pick your favorite technique for centering in your heart before making a decision. If you don't already use a technique, you can simply close your eyes, breathe deeply, and then visualize and feel a flame burning brightly in your heart. You can also recall an experience that makes you feel happy or grateful—a memory that makes the flame in your heart burn more intensely. Once you feel a sense of joy or peace, turn back to the issue at hand. Ask yourself: *What is the best way for me to resolve this issue? What is my next step?* Then listen for the answer that arises.

⑦ Find out what you're hiding from. If you have difficulty drawing necessary boundaries, don't be afraid to dig in and find out why. What do you think will happen if you don't sacrifice all the time? Are you sacrificing because you are afraid to make others unhappy by saying no? Are you addicted to sacrifice because it boosts your self-esteem to have others need you? Does sacrificing get your mind off your worries or provide an excuse for not moving ahead with your own dreams? Once you understand what has been motivating you, you can begin to challenge the myths behind these beliefs, and you'll find it easier to take the steps listed here to draw better boundaries and honor yourself.

"Know Thyself"

CHAPTER 4

ACCEPTING SUPPORT
and FLYING SOLO

*We are rich only through what we give,
and poor only through what we refuse.*
— MADAME SWETCHINE

*"My progress is my own responsibility. I do not need
others and I should not depend on them for help."* Myth
or magic?

At first blush, the answer seems obvious. As John
Donne so memorably wrote, "No man is an island, entire of itself; every man is a piece of the continent." All
the great traditions encourage us to value "the pieces"
and to therefore seek out a community of like-minded
friends who will support, inspire, and guide us. Buddhism calls it "taking refuge" in the community. The Native American Shawnee chief Tecumseh said it this way:
"A single twig breaks, but the bundle of twigs is strong."

But not so fast. It turns out that those statements are
only part of the truth. There is another, paradoxical, side

to the story. The Buddha also told his followers, "Be an island unto yourself. Take refuge *in yourself*." In Christianity, we hear "Work out your own salvation." And the Hindu Manusmriti, or Laws of Manu, like many other sources of universal wisdom, claims that "true happiness is born of self-reliance." In essence, the sages encourage us to be self-reliant *and* to seek support— to embrace both independence *and* interdependence. At times, it's important to ask for support, and at times we must fly solo. Knowing what's the right approach to take, and when, is part of the play of paradox.

We've all experienced the push-pull of this paradox before. As children and then young adults, we long to let go of our parents' apron strings as we learn, literally and figuratively, to stand on our own two feet. As adults, we may find ourselves doing the opposite. We desperately hang on to something or someone when it's really time for us, or them, to move on.

Life is always trying to bring us into balance. If we are too independent, we will find ourselves in a situation where we must collaborate in order to survive. If we are too dependent or passive, life will sooner or later cut us free from the relationships, jobs, people, or possessions that prevent us from making progress. When I was in my twenties, for instance, I worked for a time as a night-shift editor. It was a solitary kind of existence but one where I was compelled to take on more responsibility. I had to move projects forward, approve press proofs, and make critical decisions on my own.

It wasn't easy, and for a time it felt as if I had been relegated to living on the moon. Later, I came to see that the situation had been tailor-made to strengthen my weak points, especially my indecisiveness and lack of confidence. It prepared me to grow in self-reliance and ultimately to manage an entire editorial department. Like a mother bird who knows what's best for her chicks, life will nudge us out of our comfortable nests—or, if we're really stubborn, give us a swift kick in the pants—to force us to fly on our own.

A SIGN OF STRENGTH

Nature is full of metaphors that help us understand the paradox of seeking support and flying solo. Take the habit that birds have of flying together in V-shaped formations. Flying like that saves energy. It reduces the drag force the birds would experience if flying alone and permits them to fly much farther than they could by themselves. Scientists think that flying in a V formation also allows birds to communicate visually with each other during their long migrations so they won't lose members of their flock so easily. When the lead bird, who has to work the hardest, gets tired and falls back, another bird quickly takes its place. In fact, all the birds get a chance to lead. Survival during their Olympic migrations depends on individual strength *and* teamwork. They naturally integrate the skills of self-reliance and support.

For us, that kind of integration doesn't always come naturally. Some of us feel awkward asking for support. If that's the case for you, you may be burdened with the insidious myth that "if I can't make it on my own, something is wrong with me." Even worse, you may believe that you don't deserve support. Everyone deserves support, and we all must learn to give as well as receive it.

We forget that even the brightest stars in any field of endeavor have always needed their coaches, mentors, and cheerleaders. Where would the heroic hobbit Frodo Baggins be if his friend Samwise Gamgee hadn't stuck by him through thick and thin, saving Frodo several times so that he could complete his mission? How far would Helen Keller have gotten without her faithful tutor, Anne Sullivan, or Luke Skywalker without his teachers par excellence, Obi-Wan Kenobi and Yoda? How could Michael Phelps have earned his eight gold metals and an Olympic world record without teammates to help win those stunning medley relays? You are no different. Someone is destined to be your cheerleader and help you move toward the fulfillment of your dreams.

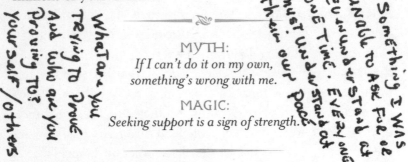

MYTH:
*If I can't do it on my own,
something's wrong with me.*

MAGIC:
Seeking support is a sign of strength.

(handwritten note, left margin): What are you Trying To Prove And who are you Proving To? yourself/others

(handwritten note, right margin): Something I was unable to ask for or understand at one Time. Everyone must understand their own pace.

One of the greatest lessons you can learn in the inner art of giving and receiving is that asking for support, when appropriate, is not a sign of weakness but a sign of strength. Asking for support is healthy. It means you believe that you are worthy of receiving. Not only that, but it's an act of love. When you seek support in making the best decisions in your life, you are acting out of love—love for yourself and for those who will be impacted by your choices.

LET US WALK TOGETHER

You may think that the effects of support are rather intangible, a touchy-feely kind of business. Yet researchers have shown that support actually increases our chances for a healthier and longer life. An early study in the 1960s is particularly fascinating. Roseto, a small, close-knit town in Pennsylvania settled by

Italian immigrants, drew the attention of researchers because the people there had lower rates of senility and a 40 percent lower rate of heart attacks, even though their diets, cholesterol levels, and other factors (such as smoking and lack of exercise) were no different than others.

What gave the people of Roseto such an advantage? Researchers pointed to their remarkable cohesiveness, mutual trust, and support. The inhabitants of this small town lived in three-generation households, they had close family and community ties, and they enjoyed their lives. What's just as intriguing is that when those factors changed, the statistics changed too. As the younger generation grew up and became more affluent, some moving away, the traditionally cohesive family and community relationships of Roseto began to erode. Coinciding with those changes, the heart attack rate in Roseto bounced up to the national average.

The sages tell us that an environment of community support is a key factor in our spiritual health as well. "Do not separate yourself from the community," advised the Jewish sage Hillel. The Eastern adept El Morya affirmed the need for a community of friends as we travel along life's way in these poetic words: "Wayfarer, friend, let us travel together. Night is near, wild beasts are about, and our campfire may go out. But if we agree to share the night watch, we can conserve our forces. Tomorrow our path will be long and we may become exhausted. Let us walk together. We shall have joy and festivity. . . . Traveler, be my friend."[1]

In Christianity, the community of friends is called the church, from the Greek word *ekklesia*, which originally meant "assembly" or "group." In Buddhism, the community is so central that it is one of the "three jewels" that a Buddhist turns to for refuge, the other two being the Buddha and the Teaching.

I like the way the Vietnamese Zen Buddhist monk Thich Nhat Hanh defines the community, which is known as the "sangha" in that tradition. The community is a group of monks and nuns as well as laymen and laywomen "who practice together to encourage the best qualities in each other," says Thich Nhat Hanh. "To me, to practice with the Sangha means to practice with those who are with you now and with those you love. . . . If it moves in the direction of transformation, it is a real Sangha."[2]

On the path of honoring yourself, I encourage you to think of your communities, your support networks, in broad ways. Community creates a space, even if it's in cyberspace, where you can receive support and give support. Your community can be your family, those you work with, those who share your spiritual or personal interests, or those you connect with to pursue creative goals or a service-oriented cause. You can be part of more than one community, because each network plays a different role in helping you honor your inner needs and share your greatest gifts. Whether you are feeling alone, need help, or want to support and serve with others, consider joining a community that shares your interests and warms your heart. If you can't find one that appeals to you, start your own!

To be clear, by "support" and "community" I'm not talking about sympathy that encourages you to wallow in self-pity, indulge in griping, or act the part of a victim. Support is something that holds you up, not keeps you down. Support is loving encouragement as well as honest feedback. Because we can't see ourselves objectively, we need true friends in the setting of community to be a mirror, to reflect back to us what our actions look like. Without interacting with others, how will you know if you are really being loving and generous or close-hearted and selfish? How will you know if you are honoring others and honoring yourself?

SPACES IN YOUR TOGETHERNESS

You honor yourself when you ask for support. Yet, like those birds on their long and arduous migrations, you also have to rely on your own inner strength to make it through. Navigating the paradox of accepting support and flying solo requires a keen sense of balance. There can be a blurred line between receiving help and allowing a helper to control your life. You'll stay in balance if you make sure you have a clear understanding of what you are expecting from those who offer help and what they expect in return. No matter what form the support comes in, remember that, in the end, it is up to you to make the decisions that directly affect you. You must be the guiding star in your life.

Even in close relationships, where mutual support should come with the territory, it's essential to strike a balance between leaning on another and standing strong and tall on your own. In one of my favorite pieces of literature, *The Prophet* by the Lebanese writer Kahlil Gibran, the beloved wise man of Orphalese addresses this need for balance. When asked to speak about marriage, he says: "Let there be spaces in your togetherness. . . . Sing and dance together and be joyous, but let each one of you be alone, even as the strings of a lute are alone though they quiver with the same music. . . . Stand together yet not too near together: for the pillars of the temple stand apart, and the oak tree and the cypress grow not in each other's shadow."[3]

The following Hasidic story also shows why self-reliance is indispensable. A young rabbi complained to his mentor that he felt full of life when he studied, but when he turned away from that source of support and went about his daily activities, this mood disappeared. "What should I do?" he asked. His astute teacher replied with an apt analogy: "You must be like the man who is walking through the forest in the dark accompanied by a friend. A time will come when the two companions must part and each must go his own way alone. Neither will fear the darkness if he carries his own lantern." When it comes down to it, you must be able to depend on yourself to light your way.

That sound advice applies to all our relationships. You will be asked to give and receive support in many ways as you walk through life. The magic takes place when everyone in the relationship, including you, is also free to realize his or her full potential. In relationships at work, see what happens when you are appreciative of support but also welcome new perspectives and encourage others to innovate. In intimate relationships, give yourself time and space to pursue the desires of your heart and soul.

MYTH:
*Constant support, togetherness, and
unanimity create the best relationships.*

MAGIC:
*My relationships are stronger when I pursue my
own interests and nurture my individual strengths.*

If you don't allow yourself to exercise your own inner muscles, your own mind, and your own heart, they will atrophy. Jessica and her mother had a rude awakening to that lesson. Jessica, in her late twenties, had a pernicious habit of overcharging her credit card. She couldn't keep her spending in line with what she could afford. That problem was bad enough, but she had another problem that was just as challenging—a mother who always bailed her out. Jessica's mother, Sharifa, would always come to her daughter's rescue and pay off her credit cards when she got into trouble.

As a single mother who raised her only daughter by herself, Sharifa was overprotective of Jessica. She thought that paying off Jessica's debts was a way of showing her love. Jessica began to feel uncomfortable about this. To her credit (no pun intended), she realized that she needed to overcome her habit of overspending if she wanted to build a solid financial future. She loved her mother, but she didn't want to depend on her for the rest of her life. She finally told her mom to stop bailing her out.

Surprisingly, this was a scarier proposition for mother than daughter. Sharifa's chief concern wasn't that Jessica would get herself into irreparable trouble. What she was really afraid of was that if Jessica became an independent adult, she might no longer need her. Sharifa was afraid that she would lose her daughter. Fortunately, the two were able to talk about this together. Jessica assured her mother that she would always love her, but she also let her mother know that she needed to become financially secure on her own.

Sharifa, like Susan, whom we met in chapter 3, was learning that sacrificing for others is not always the most effective way to love them or help them grow. Everyone has to learn to fly solo. We cannot live another person's life for them, no matter how much we love them, and they can't live ours. When we truly love, we give others the freedom to be themselves and to learn for themselves.

PROTECTING OURSELVES, WE PROTECT OTHERS

In ancient times, a bamboo acrobat, who performed feats atop a bamboo pole, took on an apprentice. The teacher instructed his young pupil to climb the pole and stand on his shoulders, saying, "You look after me and I will look after you. By watching over each other in this way, we will both be safe, make a

good profit, and be able to come down from the pole safely."
His pupil, however, disagreed. "No, master," he said, "you must
look after yourself and I must look after myself. By each of us
protecting ourselves, we'll be able to do our feats, make a good
profit, and come down from the pole safely."

Who was correct—the master or the apprentice? When the
Buddha told this tale centuries ago, he explained to his listeners
that the apprentice had the right idea. Then he uttered one of
the paradoxes that is at the heart of the inner art of giving and
receiving: *Protecting oneself, one protects others; protecting
others, one protects oneself.* Two complementary truths with
profound implications.

Like many wisdom tales, this story contains several layers of
meaning. The most obvious is one we've explored before: by
protecting yourself—by first caring for yourself and filling your
inner needs—you garner the strength to help others. That's why
we always hear on airplane flights that if there is an emergency,
we should put on our own oxygen masks first before helping
others put on theirs. If you can't breathe, how can you help others survive? If you're stuck, how can you help others get unstuck? To say it in paradoxical terms, *at times you can support
others the most by supporting yourself first.* Taking time to care
for yourself may temporarily look to others as selfish or uncar-
ing, but it's not. Increasing your capacity to give is the most giving thing you can do.

That far-reaching concept was put into action by a young
monk who, upon hearing that the Buddha was on his deathbed
and would soon pass away, retreated to his room to meditate.
He alone did not join the visitors who streamed in and out to
visit the revered teacher. The others, thinking he lacked proper
concern and respect for their leader's welfare, reported his con-
duct, and he was asked to pay a visit to the Buddha. When he

did, he explained that he had been meditating by himself because he thought the highest honor he could give his teacher would be to attain an enlightened state himself during the Buddha's lifetime.

This young man also knew that the highest honor he could give those who would look to him for support in the future would be to pull out all the stops and develop the best in himself now. He had discovered the cardinal principle that makes the art of giving and receiving come alive: *you help others most by being the greatest version of yourself you can be*. Flying solo for the moment would prepare him to lift up others on his wings of strength.

To complete the circle, we must go back to the lesson of those bamboo acrobats. In addition to saying that by "protecting oneself, one protects others," the Buddha also said, paradoxically, the very opposite: "protecting others, one protects oneself." What did he mean?

He meant, quite simply, that when we support others and treat them with loving-kindness, we protect ourselves because we are creating the kind of world we want to live in. We always get back what we put out. What goes around comes around. That's the universal law of cause and effect. One way that works is by the tremendous power of our example. By acting the way we do, we are essentially telling people: "This is how the world works—just look at my example. I act like this, so this is how I expect to be treated in return." When we are greedy, therefore, we aren't really benefiting ourselves in the long run because we are breeding greed. We are literally creating a world where eventually someone will exploit us. When, on the other hand, we act with love and kindness, we are propagating those qualities. And in that kind of world, we ourselves will be treated with love and kindness. What kind of world would you rather live in?

[handwritten margin note]: unless you want something from someone special to you and they don't or can't or do not want to treat you this way.

I recently met a waitress who lived by the principle of "protecting others, we protect ourselves." I was having dinner with a friend at a self-serve buffet, and the young woman who took our order and brought us our drinks was so cheerful and helpful that my friend wanted to make sure she received the entire tip. When he asked whether she had to share her tips with the others who worked there, she immediately replied, "We all share! If I didn't share, the others working here wouldn't share with me." With a pure heart, she instinctively knew that how she treated others would come full circle back to her. It was another reminder to me of the powerful and exacting law of the circle. By honoring others and giving them support, we are in turn honored and supported.

KEYS TO THE
BALANCING ACT

Is It Time to Seek Support or Stand on Your Own?

Every part of life, as it grows and evolves, naturally moves between seeking support and flying solo. Only when those elements are in balance do we make real and lasting progress. Leaning too much or too long in one direction or the other slows us down. The following four questions and the tips that go with them can help you target which part of the paradox needs your attention so you can get back in balance and move full steam ahead.

■ **Is there an area of your life where you are trying to make progress on your own but feel stuck?** What kind of support would help you move forward more quickly? Remember that support can be physical, mental, emotional, and spiritual. It can be anything from getting a regular massage once a week to joining a community where you can share your passion. It can involve talking through a decision with someone you trust or taking part in your favorite form of inspiration. In the spirit of giving and receiving, consider trading services with someone whose help you need. What one step can you take right now to seek support, guidance, or advice in an area where you feel stuck?

■ **Do you tend to tackle all of life's challenges by yourself?** If you have a hard time asking for help, keep reminding yourself of these two truths: First, seeking support is the loving thing to do and the strong thing to do. By getting the right help in making good decisions and taking the next step, you are honoring yourself as well as those who will be affected by your choices, now and in the future. Second, people are more willing to help than you might think. If the people you approach cannot help right now or are not willing to help, it doesn't mean you aren't worthy. It just means you haven't found the right supporters yet. You will.

■ **Are you in a personal or business relationship with someone who is making decisions that you should be making?** What would you like to tell that person about how you are feeling? What would you like to request of him or her? Try crafting what you want to say on paper first before explaining it in person. You may even need to send your message in writing so you can fully express what you find it hard to say in person. Follow up to make sure that the person you are addressing understands what you are asking and that you both have the same expectations going forward.

■ **Are there spaces in your togetherness?** Having a close relationship doesn't mean you should give up being yourself. In fact, you may get irritated with those you love simply because you need some regular time apart, some breathing space. No two people have all the same interests, and it's not healthy to expect that to be the case. Do you allow and encourage yourself and your partner to pursue your own individual interests? Take some dedicated time for yourself and allow your partner to do the same. You'll have more to offer each other and the world as a result.

PART TWO

GIVE YOURSELF AWAY
and HONOR YOUR HEART

When I give, I give myself.

—Walt Whitman

As we delve more deeply into the inner art of giving and receiving, we come to see that we don't just honor ourselves by stepping back from the busyness that surrounds us to attend to our own needs. We also honor ourselves by doing the opposite—by not holding back and by giving all we can give. To understand why this is true, we must dissect our long-held beliefs around gift-giving, many of which block us from giving the most important gift we can give—the gift of our heart. Through a creative, heart-centered approach to giving, we discover our essence. We discover what we are capable of giving. And we learn that it's not just *what* we give, but *how* and *when* we give that can make all the difference.

CHAPTER 5

BETTER THAN BIGGER

 You give but little when you give of your possessions.
It is when you give of yourself that you truly give.
—KAHLIL GIBRAN

"The one who gives is the one who receives the most.
We make a living by what we get, but we make a life by
what we give." Myth or magic? That depends on the
why, the when, and the how of our giving—and these
depend on only one thing: the heart.

In the details of our days, it's easy to lose sight of
the meaning behind the moments. It's easy to forget the
truth that giving, at its essence, is the creative activity of
the heart. We aren't just reactors but actors, not mere
imitators but creators. The words of wisdom we hear
about giving are mere platitudes unless we experience
for ourselves that giving is not about giving up or giving
in, but about giving birth—to ourselves—and creating
with the heart.

[handwritten margin note:] ARE WE Giving or doing? Is it A Task to be completed or a gift? How & what?

You are a creator. Every day, you are blessed with an allotment of energy to do with what you will. This energy makes your heart tick, keeps you breathing, and gives you the stamina to move through your day. What you choose to do with that energy as you direct it through your thoughts, feelings, and interactions with others is your gift to life.

MYTH:
Life happens, and often all I can do is react.

MAGIC:
*I am a creator. Every day I choose how to use
my creative power to shape my life and give to others.*

We tend to think that giving and receiving happens when we hand over something that is wrapped and tied with a bow and ribbon, but in reality we are always giving. We are giving birth to something every moment. When you give, you are taking the energy that the universe has so generously put at your disposal and you are endowing it with form and expression. You are stamping it, so to speak, with your personal signature, the signature of your heart. As Elizabeth Clare Prophet, a pioneer in practical spirituality, once said, "Love is the creative force and power. You are a co-creator with God. It's an awesome responsibility. What are you going to do with your power to create? What are you going to create?"

In the language of the heart, giving translates as offering a part of yourself to someone who, at that moment, needs it more than you do. By giving in this way, you not only honor others. You also honor yourself because you are allowing your heart to do what it was made to do—give and receive love. Psychologist and philosopher Eric Fromm put it this way: "Giving is the

And Time

OR Some one you want to Share with

highest expression of potency. In the very act of giving, I experience my strength, my wealth, my power. . . . Giving is more joyous than receiving, not because it is a deprivation, but because in the act of giving lies the expression of my aliveness."[1]

How can you tell when your giving is the highest expression of your aliveness? You don't have to be clairvoyant to see the form and expression your energy creations take. It's easy—simply watch their effect on others. Watch the look on the face of the salesgirl you complain to or compliment, or how your children look when they see you interact with the person who just stole your parking space.

HOW WE GIVE

You may sometimes feel as if you are being forced to give, that you have no choice, and therefore you have a right to complain. That kind of giving, more bitter than sweet, holds a valuable message for you. Grumbling, irritation, resentment, and the urge to hold back can be signals that, in some way, you aren't balancing what you give to others with what you need to give to yourself. If you find that you can't give with the fullness of your heart, don't judge yourself. When you catch yourself giving with a grudge, it's not a matter of right or wrong, good or bad. It's a matter of discovering why and adjusting the flow.

Being out of balance is just one reason we may not be able to give wholeheartedly. Another is that we have been schooled by a material culture whose long-held beliefs mask the magic that comes from giving with the heart. The Native American reformer Charles Alexander Eastman (Ohiyesa) touched on this when he said, "As a child I understood how to give. I have forgotten this grace since I have become civilized. I lived the natural life, whereas I now live the artificial."

Today, more than ever, we are showered with media messages vying to convince us to buy more and buy bigger. As little children size up their stack of birthday or holiday gifts, bigger and more always seem better. I'll never forget the sobs that came from a little niece of mine one Christmas morning when she had finished unwrapping the two gifts we had given her, only to see that her sister had an extra package from us to open. She felt cheated, even though we had carefully spent equal amounts of money on them both.

Yet take a moment and think about the times, as a child or adult, when you felt most happy, joyful, or at peace. Were those moments really defined by how much money someone spent on you? Or was it the time and attention you received or the intimacy and connection you experienced that made you feel exuberant? The wiser we become in the ways of the heart, the more we realize that the biggest and most expensive gifts aren't necessarily the best ones. Better than bigger is the gift of the heart.

MYTH:
*The bigger and more expensive the gifts
that I give—and get—the better.*

MAGIC:
Better than bigger is the gift of the heart.

One summer day, not long after my husband and I had moved into a new home, my almost five-year-old neighbor Sophie peeked through the bushes separating her backyard from mine and introduced herself. After she and I had exchanged some important facts about each other, like how old she and her sister were and the names of my kitties, she suddenly asked, "What's your favorite color?" "Well, I like yellow," I replied.

In an instant, she was off, disappearing around the side of her house and calling behind her shoulder, "Stay right there, stay right there!" When she returned, she came bearing gifts. "Here's a flower from our garden," she announced, "a yellow flower." With a smile big enough for the both of us, she stretched her arm toward me. She was carefully holding between her fingers a perfect yellow pansy.

It's been a few years since Sophie graced me with her pansy and I'm sure she's forgotten all about it. But I'll never forget her gift—and the smile that leapt from her heart and landed smack in the middle of mine. Sophie knew instinctively what the beloved classic of India, the Bhagavad Gita, has taught for millennia: "He who offers to me [God] with devotion only a leaf, or a flower, or a fruit, or even a little water, this I accept from that yearning soul, because with a pure heart it was offered with love."[2] It's not just *what* you give but *how* you give that counts. It's not the size of the gift but the size of your heart.

CAN GIFTS BE COP-OUTS?

No matter how much you spend on gifts, it doesn't make up for what your heart is doing. In fact, those big, expensive gifts can be cop-outs. We've all done it—run to a store at the last minute to get someone a gift, any gift. Or we've bought a gift that we liked and then were surprised when the person we gave it to wasn't quite so excited about it. Neither of those kinds of giving really meets the other person's needs or honors the creative spirit within us.

The most special gifts are the ones we give with our heart, not just with our head. A neighbor once mentioned to me that her husband and two children had given her the best Mother's Day gift she had ever received—a coupon for a massage. "What

All give some and some give all

a great surprise that was," she said. "I've got more than enough stuff, so I don't need more things. I told them: keep those massages coming!" Her family's gift hit its target—her heart—because they had gone into their hearts and figured out what *she* needed.

Joanie, a radio show host who had asked me to be on her show, told me how she had recently gotten creative with her gift-giving. She had been invited to a baby shower for a good friend who was expecting twins. She knew how busy life would be for her friend once the babies arrived, so she bought something for the newborns to wear and also gave her friend a one-year open invitation to call her at any time to help fold laundry. "My friend was thrilled," she said. "She appreciated that more than anything else I could have given her."

One of my special memories from childhood was how much my family appreciated my homemade birthday cards. As a child, I loved to design cards and write beautiful sentiments to my parents and sisters. I'll never forget my father and mother telling me how much they loved my creations. They encouraged me to keep making cards that had my personal touch instead of buying the glitzy generic ones from the store.

Every opportunity for gift-giving is an opportunity to give away a special part of ourselves. Margaret, for example, has been operating for most of her life on the premise that the time we share with a friend is far more important than giving or getting a physical gift. Born and raised in Ireland, she grew up in an environment where children, not adults, received gifts for holidays. One year, Margaret explained how she felt about gift-giving to Sandra, a co-worker who had become a good friend. Margaret pulled her new friend aside and bluntly told her, "It's time for me to give you the lecture I give all my friends. *Don't* get me a Christmas present or a birthday present, because I don't want one. What am I going to do with more things? If you want to go out to lunch with me, that's fine because then we get to spend time together. But if you get me a gift, you'll just have to work harder to pay for it—and then you'll have even less time to spend with me."

It was Sandra who shared this story with me. "I actually felt relieved when I heard this," she admitted, "and I appreciated my friendship with Margaret even more." Sandra went on to tell me that a few years ago for Christmas, she had decided to do something similar. She told her relatives and close friends that instead of buying them material gifts, she wanted to spend some time alone with them. "It was the best Christmas I ever had," she recalled, smiling. "I was able to spend time with all my favorite people and I wasn't rushing around shopping. I didn't even go to the mall once!"

THE GIFT OF FOCUSED ATTENTION

One of the most significant gifts we can give in this modern, busy time of ours *is* our time. With so many demands placed upon us, we often find ourselves talking or listening to someone who needs us while we are also driving, watching TV, answering our cell phones, text messaging, making dinner, going through a stack of mail, or taking in everything else going on around us. We're only half there. We're only half giving. It's impossible to be fully giving unless we are giving our full attention. That sounds simple, but how often do we do it? How often do we maintain an unbroken connection with those who need us?

The practice of focusing our attention, of being mindful and fully aware in the now, is advocated by Eastern and Western teachers alike. "You cannot succeed in loving God or your neighbor . . . if your mind is perpetually distracted," said the

Christian monastic Basil of Caesarea. To the Zen masters, full awareness of and openness to what is taking place in the moment is indispensable. A famous Zen master said it this way: "When walking, just walk. When sitting, just sit. But above all, don't wobble!"

Giving your undivided attention to another is nurturing and healing. It breeds that rare and precious commodity of true intimacy and connectedness. How can you tell when two people are deeply in love? For one, as the saying goes, lovers only have eyes for each other. Each one's gaze is fixed on the beloved—so much so that they don't notice what is going on around them. When we are locked in that warm embrace of an unbroken circle of energy, we know that at that moment we are the sole object of our partner's attention. We feel deeply loved and supported. A focused, heart-centered connection is an essential ingredient for good relationships in any setting.

I experienced the transformative power of focused attention when I was supervising the department I talked about earlier. I would be at my desk hearing about issues that needed attention and, at the same time, my phone would inevitably ring, bringing news of some urgent problem that needed to be solved. I didn't realize how exasperating and even disrespectful my taking those calls felt to my teammates until one of them pointed this out to me. I started to turn the phone off and let the calls go through to my answering machine when I was engaged in crucial or timely conversations. As a result, I was able to understand and resolve issues more quickly. More importantly, this helped create more connected and compassionate relationships. The gift of our time and our undiluted attention can create magic in any relationship, whether at home, at work, or at play.

CHAPTER 6

WHAT *and* WHEN DO WE GIVE?

"I mean, what IS an un-birthday present?"

*"A present given when it isn't your birthday, of course.
. . . There are three hundred and sixty-four days when
you might get un-birthday presents—"*
— ALICE AND HUMPTY DUMPTY

Birthdays, graduations, weddings, anniversaries, Christmas, Hanukkah, and other holidays—so many occasions to give gifts. Yet the most touching gifts are often the ones that come as *un*birthday or *un*holiday or *un*anniversary gifts.

"It is well to give when asked," wrote Kahlil Gibran, "but it is better to give unasked, through understanding."[1] How often do you stop to appreciate another's heart and give spontaneously—perhaps a bunch of flowers to celebrate a project well done, a special book to thank someone for her kindness, or a beautiful card with a personal message to cheer up a troubled friend?

People most need our gifts when they are experiencing difficulty, and yet that's when we are most tempted to withhold them. We take their churlish complaints or temper tantrums personally, when these are really SOS calls for support. "What's wrong with you?" we mutter, instead of asking, "Why are you hurting, and what can I do to help you?" Mother Teresa, in the framework of her deep devotion, captured that dynamic way of giving in the daily prayer for her children's home, which reads in part: "Dearest Lord, may I see you today and every day in the person of your sick, and, whilst nursing them, minister unto you. Though you hide yourself behind the unattractive disguise of the irritable, the exacting, the unreasonable, may I still recognize you."[2]

- - - ❧ - - -

MYTH:
Special occasions are the time for gift giving.

MAGIC:
Giving an unexpected gift works magic. It opens the heart of those who receive my gifts and it opens my heart.

Sometimes the best gifts are the ones that violate the very rules we have learned about giving, as this story handed down from the desert fathers, the Christian monks who lived as hermits in the deserts of Egypt, demonstrates. It tells of two young monks who once asked Abba Poemen what he thought they should do if they caught other monks asleep during prayer time. "Shouldn't we pinch them to make them stay awake?" said the monks, bothered by this apparent disrespect of their holy ritual. "Well," replied their more seasoned brother, "if I come across a brother who is sleeping, I place his head on my knees and let him rest."

SURRENDERING TO THE INSTINCTS OF THE HEART

A story from the Hindu tradition also teaches about giving from the heart in a way that meets another's unspoken need. A young spiritual seeker (who later became a beloved Indian teacher himself) was severely scolded by his teacher for failing to complete an errand properly. A more advanced student who was there at the time noticed the young man's dismay and confusion and said, "Do you know why your teacher is so hard on you?"

The young man admitted that the scolding seemed undeserved and said he did not see how he was to blame. The older disciple then explained to him that there are three classes of students. The third-class student merely obeys his teacher's bidding, he said. The second-class student doesn't have to be instructed to do something; he intuits his teacher's need as soon as the thought arises in the teacher's mind. The first-class student, however, acts even before the teacher has had time to think of his or her need.[3]

Just as an athletic coach pushes his players beyond their comfort zone so that they will become strong and excel at their sport, so the stern teacher in this story wanted his young pupil to become not only an average giver but a first-class one. He wanted him to learn how essential it is in all relationships to open our hearts and anticipate what others need, which is why he was so adamant in driving home that lesson.

Life calls each of us to surrender to that same instinct of the heart, to become so highly attuned to another's need that we are ready instruments of healing and comfort. These aren't lofty, unreachable goals. In your own way, you will always have something to give, whether a generous smile of encouragement, words of appreciation, a helping hand, a special perspective or skill, or simply a willingness to listen. You have a role to play within your sphere of influence, and your heart will show you what to give, how to give, and when to give. You just have to listen.

YOU'RE ALWAYS TEACHING SOMEONE

"Mom, I want to be just like you when I grow up," Tara told her mother as they were driving home in the car one day. Her mother was skillfully weaving in and out of traffic in the same way that she negotiated the myriad details that made up her days. "Why do you want to be like me?" her mother asked. "Well, I like the way you get things done," the little girl said.

"I had a talk with my daughter when we got home," her mom later told me. Yes, she was an expert at juggling lots of balls at once, including being a single mother, working full time at a high-powered career, and handling the emergencies of her job that popped up at any hour of the day or night. But that was not the most important thing she wanted to teach her daughter. "I explained to my little girl that there was more to life than 'getting things done.' I wanted her to know that what we do with our hearts, how we treat other people, is even more important."

Whether we realize it or not, we are teaching all the time, and the little ones in our lives are especially receptive. Children, as you can see by watching any two-year-old, love to imitate. They take in far more than meets the eye. In fact, Dr. Maria Montessori, the first woman in Italy to receive a medical degree and the founder of the Montessori method of education, coined the term "absorbent mind" to describe children up to the age of six, who, like sponges, absorb everything around them.

I remember stopping at a street corner one day at the same time that a woman and her two children were waiting there to cross the street. The signal flashed its warning not to cross, but my friend and I were in a hurry and we tiptoed to the edge of the curb, stretching our necks forward to see if we could beat the traffic and scurry safely to the other side of the street. The woman turned to us and gently said, "That wouldn't be a good example." We looked down to see two little bodies and two big pairs of eyes peering up at us. I think twice now at traffic lights.

It's not only children who watch and absorb, though. It's anyone—and everyone. You may not think of yourself as an example to others, but the wisdom teachers tell us that life, even in spiritual realms, is organized so that we are always playing the role of both student and teacher. There are people in your life you are meant to teach as well as those you are meant to learn from. Your attitude, your words, your behavior, your actions—all these set the example for someone. Whether you are standing at a bus stop, attending a meeting, picking up your children from school, or waiting in a long line of impatient caffeine aficionados at Starbucks, you are teaching and you are giving.

———— 🐚 ————

MYTH:
My everyday actions don't impact others much.

MAGIC:
What I give and how I give can change the world—
and I am always giving and teaching by my example.

If you think that your smallest actions and reactions have little or no effect, think again. Just as scientists tell us about the "butterfly effect"—that a butterfly flapping its wings in Louisiana can eventually create a tsunami in Southeast Asia—so the sages remind us that what we do and how we do it can literally change the world. Liu I-ming, an eighteenth-century Taoist, expressed that sentiment when he wrote: "A sage said, 'If for one day you can master yourself and return to considerate behavior,

[handwritten margin note:] They also send a message to others. I am too busy for you equals you are not important to me. Actions do speak louder than words.

So you can, give Fully & Freely to others.
without holding back.

80   Give Yourself Away and Honor Your Heart

the whole world will return to humanity.' Do you think humanity depends on yourself or on others? This is indeed the subtle point of this passage."[4]

GIVING WHAT YOU ARE

How we live is our greatest offering to the world. That is the crux of the matter. Cardinal Désiré-Joseph Mercier, the popular cardinal who resisted the German occupation of Belgium in World War I, said it simply and beautifully: "We must not only give what we *have*; we must also give what we *are*."

An old story, perhaps from India, makes just that point. One day, a woman traveling alone in the mountains discovered a precious stone in a stream and placed it in the pack she was carrying with her. Later, she came upon a man who had been walking for days through the mountains and was hungry. She graciously opened her pack to share her food with him, and the man could not help but notice her find. He realized that this was no mere stone but a gem worth so much that he could sell it and live off the money for the rest of his life. He asked the woman if she would give him the stone. She immediately reached into the bag, pulled out the gem, and handed it to him. Off he went with the treasure, smiling at his turn of fortune.

A few days later, as the woman continued her journey, she once again crossed paths with the man. He had retraced his steps and was running toward her, stone in hand. "Wise woman," he said, "thank you for the gift of this precious gem. It is very valuable. But I am returning it to you because I want to ask you for an even greater gift. Please give me whatever it is within you that let you give away this stone to me." Like this wise woman, who you are will inspire others far more than anything you can ever say.

1) If for some reason you are not comfortable with yourself, you can at give Loving gift you can give someone is just that. Love and accept yourself, and realize the most Loving gift you can give. Love Add Accept yourself.

CHAPTER 7

THE MAGIC *of* FLOW

Everything is yours, but on the one infinitely
important condition: that it is all given.
—THOMAS MERTON

In a culture where success and status are defined by the price we pay for cars, clothes, homes, vacations, and the latest technological gadgets, it's hard to keep in mind that happiness and success are not a consequence of the things we can buy and the number of zeroes at the end of their price tags. Yet it's vitally important that we do. Our children need to learn from us that the incessant gathering of more things does not produce more happiness.

In his classic *I'm OK—You're OK*, Dr. Thomas A. Harris suggests that our "clamoring for something *bigger, better,* and *more*" all comes from the desire of the vulnerable child within us to feel more OK. He says that even as adults, we carry around the hidden belief we took on as children that we are simply not OK. Long after the childhood events that made us feel this way are over, we may continue to accumulate more and more material goods to ward off those feelings. Surrounding ourselves with more belongings can be our way of trying to shut out the fear of being unloved, abandoned, disliked, cheated, or made fun of. In the process, though, we may become like the confused child Harris describes who was asked on a children's television program what he got for Christmas. "I don't know," said the bewildered little boy, "there was too many."[1]

If how much we amass could really make us happy, we wouldn't be hearing about so many of the rich and famous who are addicted, depressed, or destructive. Social psychologist David Myers has written about the real factors that do and do not make us happy, surveying thousands of studies conducted worldwide in the process. The findings are not what you might think. He tells us that the per-person income in America in 2002 was more than double what it was in 1957, adjusted for inflation. This wealth has enabled Americans to buy twice as many material goods, but are we more happy as a result? In one of the giant paradoxes of our time, the answer is no.

Not only are we are not happier, says Myers, but today there are twice as many divorces, almost three times as many teen suicides, and the number of people who experience depression has rocketed. He says that in Europe, Australia, and Japan it's also true that increases in income have not brought more happiness.[2] Myers believes that there are far more important factors that lead to happiness, such as living in the moment, resting, taking control of our time, and cultivating close relationships, to name a few.[3] Interestingly, those factors clearly point back to a healthy habit of honoring yourself.

Money magazine columnist Jean Chatzky surveyed over 1,500 people for her book *You Don't Have to Be Rich* and also found that money doesn't play as big a role in happiness as we think. Her research showed that having enough money for things like housing, groceries, transportation, and vacation was important, but once a family's income reaches a certain level, more money doesn't make people happier.[4]

GETTING AND LETTING GO

The enlightened ones of all cultures long ago saw through the myth that happiness and success are defined by the size of our pocketbooks. The reality, they discovered, is that happiness and success depend on the all-important factor of flow.

As we look at nature at work around us, we see a world that naturally and continuously gives and receives, gets and lets go. We are in harmony with that universal flow when we do the same—when we realize that we are meant to share what has been given to us. That's *why* it has been given to us. As Glückel of Hameln wisely wrote in a memoir she began creating for her children in late seventeenth-century Germany, "Nothing is our own, everything is only a loan." What we do with life's "loans" is what determines how much we will keep getting.

In your life, you have been assigned certain resources, whether they come in the form of opportunities, money, connections, talents, or material goods. You have been entrusted with these gifts. Sharing and making good use of what you have received automatically brings more into your life. Why is this so? Simply put, as you show that you can be trusted to wisely use both your inner and outer resources, the universe will loan you even more. It's like convincing the bank to loan you more money because you have established good credit, or like showing your boss that you can be trusted to oversee a large project because you have excelled at managing smaller ones.

That same principle is explored in the cryptic parable of the talents, where Jesus compares the fate of three different servants who are given "talents" to care for while their master is away on a trip (a talent was a unit of currency in his day). When the master returns, he finds that two of the servants—one to whom he gave five talents and one to whom he gave two talents—have doubled the money they were given. "Well done," the master tells them. "You have been faithful with a few things; I will put you in charge of many things."

The third servant, however, who received just one talent, confesses that he buried it for safekeeping because he was afraid. The master chides him for not having made better use of the money by putting it in the bank to earn interest. Then he commands that that man's money be taken from him and given to the servant who earned the most, saying, "To everyone who has, more shall be given, and he will have an abundance." This meaningful, if somewhat enigmatic, metaphor is not so hard to understand if you look at it as a lesson in the inner art of giving and receiving. It invites every one of us to look into our hearts and ask ourselves: What am I doing with my "talents"? Am I hiding them, or am I putting them to good use so that they bear fruit within my circle of influence? Am I selfishly keeping to myself the gifts that have been loaned to me, or am I freely giving my gifts and receiving even more in return?

Giving wisely and well, then, aligns us with a fundamental law that governs how the world operates. It is, of course, another paradox: *The more we give away, the more we get.* The more we increase the flow of giving and receiving in our lives, the more we have flowing. It's like priming a pump. As Anne Morrow Lindbergh once said, "The more one gives, the more one has to give—like milk in the breast."

By that definition, abundance goes hand in hand with a hearty impulse to give. True "success," you could say, is characterized by the abundant flow that moves through our lives because we are willing to share what we have received—our resources, our talents, our time, and even the lessons we have learned. We keep on getting more because we keep on giving to others what we have received.

MYTH:
The more I keep for myself, the more I will have.

MAGIC:
The more I give away, the more I will get.

In fact, interesting statistical research, hard data, shows that giving does stimulate wealth, not only for individuals but also for nations. Arthur C. Brooks, an expert on economics and public policy, reviewed that data and found that those who give more actually do earn more *as a result of their giving*. He said, "More giving doesn't just correlate with higher income; it causes higher income. And not just a little." He also pointed to findings that show that after people are seen behaving charitably, they are given leadership positions.[5]

EXERCISING YOUR HEART MUSCLE

The more you exercise your heart muscle by giving and receiving, the better it performs. When your heart is fit, your giving and receiving becomes as natural as the rhythm of your breath, in and out, over and over and over again. A wonderful friend of mine was a living example of how opening our hearts to freely give and receive increases our capacity to do more of the same.

When I first met Richard, he was in his fifties and had already gone through three open-heart surgeries, nine bypasses, and twenty other heart procedures. The doctors dubbed him "the walking miracle." Richard was a buoyant soul, and you would never know that his life was literally hanging by a thread. He couldn't be sure from one day to the next if his heart would hold out. Yet he wasn't needy or anxious. He was one of the most genuinely heartful, peaceful, and generous people I've ever known. The challenges facing his physical heart only made him more keenly aware of what his inner heart could do. He loved his daily spiritual meditations on the heart, and he was always grateful for the opportunity to put his love into action. He was so blessed in return.

Richard owned a health food store. There was something magical about the place. It was growing by leaps and bounds and was bursting at the seams. He was the first to admit that this growth wasn't a consequence of business savvy. "I don't know the first thing about running a business," he confessed to me. It was clear, however, to anyone who watched him in action that he did know the key to a thriving business: service. His business was booming because he loved to help the people who came to him looking for ways to preserve their health. His store was his way of giving.

When I would call Richard on the phone, I would often catch him working late at his desk at the back of the store, tending to the details that made everything run smoothly. In our conversations, he would never fail to tell me about a loving interaction he had had with his little granddaughter, another family member, an employee, one of his customers, or someone he had met along life's way. He relished the unseen but very palpable heart connections he shared with others.

Day by day, Richard was living with the truth that most of us do everything we can to run away from—the truth that our days are numbered. He got lots of practice reflecting on what was as relevant for him as it is for any of us: *Today might be the last day I can give and receive in this setting, in this way, and with these particular people. What will I give?* To Richard, every day was an opportunity to reach into his heart and come out with a gift of love. Every day was an opportunity to increase his capacity to give. I believe that's what kept him alive for so long and what gave him such joy.

―――――― 🕊 ――――――

MYTH:
*My happiness and success are determined
by how much I am able to get.*

MAGIC:
*True happiness and success depend not on
my ability to get more but on my capacity to
give more—my capacity to create flow.*

To me, Richard was the embodiment of what the sage Lao Tze, the prince of paradox, said about giving: "The sage has no need to hoard. When his own last scrap has been used up on behalf of others, he has more than before. The more he gives to others, the more he possesses of his own."[6] I miss you, dear friend. Thank you for teaching me about the ways of the heart.

MONEY MISCONCEPTIONS

While the sages' parables about money and success can be seen as metaphorical, there is no reason we shouldn't also take them literally. The universal truth that "the more we give away, the more we get" applies to our finances too. The idea that the enlightened ones disdain abundance is not true. They do warn about the dangers of greed—of desiring wealth only for what it can bring us—rather than seeing money as an instrument to do good and help others. But it's not money, they say, that's a concern; it's our *relationship* to money. That oft-quoted biblical passage doesn't say that money is the root of all evil. It says that "the love of money is the root of all evil" and that coveting money is what can bring us many sorrows.[7]

The misconception that money in itself is tainted is related to another subtle myth that you may find lurking below the surface, silently holding you back—the myth that whatever is physical or material is "bad" and only that which is spiritual is "good." Yet the wise ones tell us that the spiritual and material aspects of life go together. They are interconnected, integrated, and interdependent.

You can think of it like this: see the material world as a flute, and the spirit as the breath that plays the flute (the word *spirit* actually comes from *spiritus*, Latin for "breath" or "inspiration"). The flute is nothing more than a hollow piece of wood or metal until the creative spirit uses it to play its song. As importantly, the spirit needs the physical instrument to give expression to its beautiful melodies. The intangible spirit can only become tangible and express itself in this world through us. The inner world and the outer world need each other to fulfill their potential.

Looking at it in this way, why would material things, in and of themselves, be bad? It is completely natural for us to use our physical resources to express our spiritual nature and share our inner gifts. The magic of flow takes place when you take full advantage of the physical platform you've been given to put your love into action, and there is nothing more spiritual than that.

Sometimes we think that being spiritual happens only on the weekends when we're in a place of worship, or that we can only give of our spiritual self when we are praying or meditating. Those rituals certainly do help us bank our inner fires and get reconnected. But the sages say we severely limit ourselves by believing that spirituality is not a part of everyday life or by thinking that we must remove ourselves from the world (or become a hermit on a mountaintop) to be spiritual or give spiritually. The spiritual part of us is with us all the time, and we can express it at any time—no matter where we are or what we are doing.

Your everyday life is the instrument through which you express your true nature and your spirituality. Being spiritual is not escaping from the craziness of the world to slip into nirvana but integrating with the physical world to transform the craziness. What you choose to do in the most ordinary moments of the day defines what kind of giver you are.

From this perspective, money and material things are not negatives; they are tools. After all, it takes money to sustain ourselves—to have shelter, clothing, and food. It takes money to build orphanages, schools, and hospitals and to help people who are less fortunate than we are. We can do many good works with our abundance when we use that abundance from the heart. Yet we may unwittingly block abundance from coming into our lives when we harbor the attitude, at conscious or subconscious levels, that money is "bad" or even "filthy."

You are meant to have all the abundant resources you need to fulfill your role in life. Welcome those resources. Invite more of them into your life. Don't put a limit on what you can receive or how you can give. By wisely giving yourself away and honoring your heart, those resources will continue to flow.

WHO BENEFITS WHEN YOU GIVE?

Traditions around the world promote the ideal of charity, and not only because it helps those who are in need. The act of giving is as essential for the giver as it is for the receiver. We gain when we open our hearts and give ourselves away. The branch of Buddhism known as Mahayana Buddhism, for instance, encourages generosity because it increases the giver's capacity for compassion. In that tradition, giving (*dana* in Sanskrit) is the first of six *paramitas*, or perfections, to be practiced on the spiritual path.

Likewise, zakat, or giving a portion of one's wealth as alms or charity, is one of the five pillars of Islam in some braches of that tradition. In Judaism, tzedakah (charity in the sense of giving aid and money to the needy or to a worthy cause) is considered one's duty. In the Christian tradition, the apostle Paul extolled charity above even faith and hope, saying "charity never fails," and the famous Prayer of Saint Francis affirms that "it is in giving that we receive."

In addition, the principle of giving is embedded in the Judeo-Christian tradition of tithing (from the Old English word meaning "tenth"). Tithing is giving 10 percent of one's income back to God. In effect, tithing is saying "thank you" to your source of spiritual nourishment. It is based on this simple idea: *giving back to life is life-giving.* The Bhagavad Gita, from the Hindu tradition, agrees: "Nourish the gods and the gods will nourish thee," it says. "He who enjoys what is given by them without giving to them in return is truly a thief."[8]

These principles are not theoretical but highly practical, and it's not hard to put them to the test. You've probably done it yourself without even realizing it. Have you ever cleaned out your closet and given away what you no longer needed, and suddenly something new, something you did need, came into your life? It doesn't matter whether it's giving away old clothes, volunteering to help others, or ending an unhealthy relationship. Nature naturally abhors a vacuum. Whenever we create one, it will be filled. We may not always get back exactly what we expect, but the energy we offer through our gifts *will* return to us, often multiplied.

At a critical time in my life, when I had lost a job and was going through a period of intense challenge and trial, I found myself in a cycle of cutting back, letting go, and giving away. I cleaned out my closets and donated bags of clothes to the Salvation Army. I vigorously chopped away at overgrown bushes and shrubs in my yard. On my knees, I ruthlessly pulled weeds from my garden and lawn. I even cut my hair shorter. I offered more of my time to work with a nonprofit organization.

It was a difficult time for me but a healing one. It signaled the end of one season of my life and the beginning of another. Those physical actions were just the outer manifestation of what was taking place within me—clearing out the old and getting rid of clutter so I could see more clearly and make room for new growth. Slowly but surely, I created an open space, which allowed wonderful opportunities, new friendships, and needed changes to appear in my life.

KEYS TO THE
BALANCING ACT

Six Tools for Honoring
Your Heart through Giving

You honor your reason for being when you let your heart give in ways that quicken another's heart. You don't have to spend a lot of money to be a good giver. It's your inner gifts, the ones that touch another, heart to heart, that are the most precious offerings. Here are six tools that can help you create more authentic and intimate connections as you practice giving creatively, wisely, and from the heart.

1 Ask different questions. When someone in your life is being irascible, sullen, or standoffish, catch your impulse to criticize, jump to conclusions, or ask condescendingly, "What's wrong with you?" Ask more helpful questions, such as *"Why are you hurting and what can I do to help you right now?"* You can't solve others' problems for them, but you can help them understand what they are feeling and encourage them to articulate their needs. Open your heart and give by taking the opportunities that come your way to help the people in your life discover their hidden needs.

2 Give unbirthday gifts. Do you only think about giving gifts on special occasions or when you are expected to give? Try showing up with spontaneous, unbirthday gifts to let others know how much you appreciate them or to soothe the heart of someone in pain. Giving simple, spur-of-the-moment gifts from your heart will also help you to keep your own heart wide open, increasing your capacity to give and to receive even more.

❸ Be creative with your gifts. Rather than buying a present for someone at the last minute, think ahead and allow yourself to get inspired. Go into your heart and ask yourself what would really touch the heart of the person you will be giving to. (Hint: if you can't figure it out, ask them what they would like to receive!) Remember that the best gifts aren't the biggest or most expensive. Consider spending quality time with someone as your gift. If you have more than one child or sibling in your family, think about giving him or her a one-on-one date with you. The possibilities are endless.

❹ Give your full attention. Do you make yourself available to those who need you, or do you multitask—answering the phone, text messaging, or surfing the TV—while your co-worker, friend, partner, or child is trying to have a conversation with you? Giving your focused attention is an unparalleled gift that tells the people in your life that you honor them. Draw a circle around your conversations. Do what it takes to sustain the circuit of energy between you and the person you are with. Simply turning off the TV, phone, or BlackBerry and looking into someone's eyes as you listen or share can transform a situation. It shows that you care enough to be completely present.

❺ Share your life wisdom. Every one of us has a particular wisdom that we have garnered through our life experiences. Drawing from your well of wisdom to help others can be like offering a cool cup of water to someone who has been suffering from a long, agonizing thirst. Do you intentionally pass on your wisdom? If you don't know where to start, think about a challenging experience that taught you something valuable or an insight from an article, a program, or even this book that spurred a transformational moment for you. Share that insight with someone you think would benefit from your experience.

⑥ Let go and invite flow. If the magic of flow isn't happening in your life as you would like it to, go back to this simple formula: "I compel something new to come into my life by giving something away." Try cleaning out a closet and dropping off old clothes to the Salvation Army store. Instead of whittling away time on an unfruitful relationship, commitment, or habit (like watching too much TV), find a way to help someone who needs support. Consider offering your professional services gratis to a good cause. Invite your children to round up old toys and books and help them donate these items to a local charity. Watch what happens when you get rid of the clutter and open a space that you dedicate with intention to the flow of giving and receiving what you want in your life. Generosity of the heart never goes unanswered.

PART THREE

FREE YOURSELF
and HONOR ENDINGS

The beginning and the end
reach out their hands to each other.

—CHINESE PROVERB

"Stay open and receptive to everything that comes your way" has become one of the mantras of our time. Sages, psychologists, and even our best friends recite it to us. Take your hands away from your eyes and welcome whatever walks into your world, they tell us. Resist the temptation to run or hide. Honor everything and everyone in your life as a message or a messenger. It's true that we are meant to learn from the events, encounters, and emotions that take their turns tiptoeing or tramping through our lives. But does that mean we must embrace everything that shows up at our doorsteps, no matter what it looks like, feels like, or smells like? Therein lies the paradox—and where there is paradox, the magic can't be far behind.

CHAPTER 8

EYES WIDE OPEN

Honesty is the best policy,
I will stick to that.
　　　　　—SANCHO PANZA IN *DON QUIXOTE*

"I must accept everything that comes my way with open arms." Myth or magic?

At one time or another, all of us will face people or circumstances that, given the chance, would run right over us. Does our commitment to being kind and loving mean we should let them? While the world's luminaries encourage us to open up to everyone whose footprints cross our path, that's not the whole story. Paradoxically, they also give us this surprising advice: don't open your door to everyone who comes knocking.

Accepting everything that comes your way is like finding robbers outside your bedroom window and inviting them to come in through the front door and have the run of the house. You wouldn't do that, so why would you grant marauders free play with your energy and emotions?

We don't always notice the robber's approach, though. We may enter into a relationship or grab an opportunity, thinking it will finally bring us what we're looking for, only to end up feeling cheated, betrayed, and confused. Those kinds of relationships and opportunities do serve a purpose, even though they may be deeply disappointing. They force us to get to know ourselves better. They help us clarify what we do and do not want in our lives. They show us, as many times as it takes, that in order to honor ourselves we must also keep our eyes wide open.

WALKING THE LINE

Being open and kind does not mean we should put ourselves in harm's way. There is a difference between open-heartedness and foolishness, and the sages advise us to carefully walk the line between the two. When that great teacher of peace, Jesus, sent his disciples out into the world "as sheep in the midst of wolves," he told them, paradoxically, to be as "harmless as doves" but also as "wise as serpents." We hear about him teaching that when people hit us on one cheek, we should turn the other cheek to them as well. But don't forget that he also warned us to be on guard and to protect ourselves. "Beware of men," he taught. "Do not give what is holy to dogs, and do not throw your pearls before swine or they will trample them under their feet, and turn and tear you to pieces."

When to keep giving and when to put an end to a hurtful situation is not, therefore, a neat formula that we can apply in the same way to every situation. It requires discernment to know what will bring about the greatest good. A story from the Eastern tradition portrays that decision point in an unusual way. A young woman was studying with a meditation teacher to learn how to generate loving-kindness. After she performed her daily

[handwritten margin note: TRUST - BUT VERIFY And look at what motivates Them. What are They after? money - power - influence...?]

meditation practice in her home, she would walk to the market, where each day she was met with the inappropriate advances of one of the merchants. Although she tried as hard as she could to maintain love in her heart for all beings, her patience was wearing thin with this rude man.

One day, the girl became so upset that she chased the rascal down the road, wielding her umbrella over her head. Then, out of the corner of her eye, she spotted her meditation teacher walking on the other side of the road, quietly watching the scene unfold. Ashamed, she walked over to him, explaining what had happened. She told him that she felt like a failure. Her teacher, in the kind, gentle way he was known for, said that the next time something like that happened, she should go within and gather an extraordinary amount of love in her heart—and then take her umbrella and strike the scoundrel right over the head![1]

Just because we want to be loving does not mean we should become someone's doormat. The meditation teacher knew this. He knew that his young pupil could not cultivate the quality of loving-kindness without also honoring and loving herself. And she certainly wasn't honoring herself by permitting this hooligan to intrude where he didn't belong. Not only that, but by allowing this man to overstep proper boundaries, she was inviting resentment and even hatred toward him to enter her heart, the very opposite of the loving-kindness she was trying so hard to embody. At a practical level, if she didn't resist his advances, the merchant would continue to mistreat her.

In addition, the young girl wasn't doing the merchant any favors by tolerating his vile behavior. By letting him continue his shenanigans, she was inflating his ego and his false sense of entitlement. She was allowing his unhealthy habits to keep growing, to his detriment and hers. As I touched on earlier, we do not help others or ourselves when we passively accept their abuse, whether it's emotional abuse, physical aggression, blatant criticism, subtle put-downs, or any action (or inaction) that devalues our true worth. At times, the highest form of giving—of loving—is to free yourself from what's hurtful by saying no and moving out of the way. *NO IS AN ACCEPTABLE ANSWER!*

HONESTY DELIVERED WITH LOVE

There is no question that we can benefit when we look for the nugget of truth embedded in a painful situation. Another's words or actions, though harsh or spiteful, can awaken us to an aspect of our own behavior that we have refused to admit is there. At the same time, remember that not everything directed *at* you is about you. Sometimes it's not about you at all. The other person may simply be struggling with an internal battle that is spilling over into your life.

In cases like that, you can honor yourself by not taking an attack personally and not blaming yourself for another's inappropriate actions. If the shoe fits, wear it; but if it's not your shoe that's been flung at you, you don't have to pretend that it is. You don't even have to try it on. People's labels for you are not the real you. Those labels only define you if you accept them. An African proverb sums it up nicely: "It's not what you call me, but what I answer to." You can also think about that truth by asking yourself this question: Can anyone really dishonor me if I honor myself?

A scene from the life of the Buddha addresses that question with wonderful clarity. A skeptical man once heard about the Buddha and thought to himself, "I wonder if it's really true that he will still love those who abuse him and always return good for evil. I will set out and see." Upon arriving at the place where

"As A Man Thinketh in his heart, So he is." Proverbs

the Buddha was staying, the man walked up to him and began to attack him verbally, spewing out his harsh criticism and abuse. The Buddha calmly listened, and when his accuser had finally stopped his tirade, he asked him a simple question.

"If someone declined to accept a present offered to him, to whom would it belong?" he asked.

"It would belong to the person who offered the gift," the man replied.

"My son," said the Buddha, "you have railed at me, but I decline to accept your abuse and ask you to keep it yourself. Will it not be a source of misery to you? As the echo belongs to the sound, and the shadow to the substance, so misery will overtake the evil-doer without fail."

Then he continued his teaching with two fitting analogies: "A wicked person who reproaches a virtuous one is like one who looks up and spits at heaven; the spittle doesn't soil the heaven but comes back and defiles him. The slanderer is like one who flings dust at another when the wind is blowing toward himself; the dust returns on him who threw it. The virtuous person cannot be hurt, and the misery that the other would inflict comes back on himself." Hearing these words, the man realized how foolish he had been and walked away. Later, he returned to learn more and join the Buddha's community.[2]

It may seem that this story is about the accuser and how he was transformed by hearing a wise man's words. In reality, it is also a profound lesson on how to appropriately respond to abuse. Had the Buddha believed his attacker's criticism, he might have begun to doubt himself. He might have accepted everything the man had to say, in effect giving his attacker permission to define him. He could have become outraged and lashed out at his attacker, which would only have infuriated the man further and escalated the conflict. In either case, by over-reacting the Buddha would have lost his perspective and his ability to see the truth. Instead, he took the opportunity to stand up for himself, go into his heart, and deliver with love the truth this man needed to hear. In so doing, he honored himself and liberated his attacker.

MYTH:
In order to be loving, I must embrace everything that comes my way with open arms.

MAGIC:
At times, the most loving thing I can do is say no and move out of the way.

That story holds yet another valuable lesson for us. It shows that love is not wishy-washy or passive. Even when we are drawing the line and putting an end to an unhealthy situation, we can do it in a way that is frank and firm as well as loving and considerate. How we do something is as important as what we do. The Buddha didn't take the bait and accuse his attacker of being a horrible person, but he did make it clear that he would not accept abuse. Because he refused to accept the man's criticism or take his words personally, the insults didn't stick. By delivering his message with honesty and love, the Buddha, in effect, stepped out of the way and held up a mirror so the man could see for himself the truth that his abusive behavior would not hurt its target but, in the end, would only harm himself.

Honoring ourselves and others in that way gives us tremendous power because what we say comes not from the defensive ego but from a heart filled with love and goodwill. As the Buddha put it, "If a man foolishly does me wrong, I will return to him the protection of my ungrudging love." Honesty delivered with love is a gift. By honestly and lovingly drawing the line, by choosing not to accept someone's harmful behavior, we honor ourselves *and* we uphold the best and the highest in that person. Shakespeare's familiar lines were never more germane: "This above all: to thine own self be true, and it must follow, as the night the day, thou canst not then be false to any man."

CHAPTER 9

BEING HONEST
about YOUR FEELINGS

We reason deeply when we forcibly feel.
—MARY WOLLSTONECRAFT

Honor and *honest*. Both words can be traced back to the Latin word *honos*, meaning honor or dignity. It may not seem that they share much more in common, but if you dig deeper, you'll see why they do. We cannot truly *honor* ourselves unless we are first *honest* with ourselves.

Honesty comes from a deep self-knowing, a knowing that resides in the heart, in the soul, in the gut. Some of us grew up with layers of "musts" and "shoulds" that are in open warfare with what our heart and intuition are trying to tell us. In your formative years, you may have been told that expressing your feelings was a sign of weakness, that feelings aren't valid, or that crying is for babies. Your feelings may have gone into hiding when you heard phrases like "Stop complaining," "Be quiet," or "Don't be silly—there's nothing to cry about."

OR directed By Parents, Church and other Authority Figures. Control & direct your Thoughts AND actions

You may have been taught the stoic approach: set your feelings aside because someone else's needs take priority over your own.

All those messages create tension and confusion, making it hard to accept that both sides of the paradox—giving to others *and* giving to yourself—are equally valid. As a result of living with this confusion, you may have a hard time being honest with yourself when someone or something in your life is unhealthy. You may allow what you feel or intuit ("this hurts" or "something doesn't feel right") to be immediately drowned out by what you think is expected of you ("be strong," "don't flinch," or "hey, get over it"). That can be dangerous.

To give a simplistic example, if you put your hand too close to a hot stove, you will feel pain and yank your fingers away. If you didn't sense the heat, you wouldn't know that you were in danger of getting badly burned. In situations that are far less black and white, your feelings are the sensory organs of your soul, warning you of more than physical danger. If you're not in touch with your feelings, how will you know when you're about to get burnt in a one-sided relationship? If you don't allow yourself to feel upset or violated, how will you know when it's time to draw boundaries? If you don't feel compassion for others, how will you know when it's time to spring into action to help them?

Your feelings are an integral part of your internal guidance system. Yes, their kicking and screaming may at times get out of hand. And, yes, there are situations where you are called to rise to the occasion and give heroically, even if your emotions kick up a fuss. That does not, however, mean that you should throw a wet blanket over your feelings whenever they try to surface. It's essential to evaluate your feelings as you would any other piece of information you gather so you can make an emotionally intelligent choice in every situation. Logic alone won't get you there. In the words of the Bengali poet Rabindranath

Tagore, "A mind all logic is like a knife all blade. It makes the hand bleed that uses it."[1]

LETTING YOURSELF SEE

Swami Vivekananda, a renowned nineteenth-century spiritual leader and reformer who did much to introduce Eastern ideas to the Western world, once said, "Who makes us ignorant? We ourselves. We put our hands over our eyes and weep because it is dark."[2] When you give yourself permission to feel, you are taking your hands away from eyes and letting yourself see.

I learned an important lesson about the role of my feelings in the way we all learn best, by experiencing firsthand what happens when we shut them out. I had been working with someone on a project for over two years. It seemed like a wonderful opportunity and I had jumped wholeheartedly into the project without asking a lot of questions or making sure we were both on the same page about financial outcomes. I was freelancing at the time and decided to cut back on my workload so I could devote a lot of my time to this venture.

As the months rolled by, I found myself doing the lion's share of the work when I had assumed we would be taking equal responsibility up front. At times, my partner didn't show up for our scheduled meetings and didn't let me know ahead of time that he was going to miss them. When I told him this wasn't working for me, he promised that these things would change with the same exuberance that had attracted me to the project in the first place. Knowing that he did have a good heart and that we shared a passion for this work, I stuck with it. Besides, I had already invested so much time into this. So I suppressed my doubts, slamming the lid over my unease every time it whispered, waved, or even held up its pinky finger. I kept telling myself,

"That feeling in my stomach can't be right. This is a great opportunity. Be quiet!"

As my partner began making decisions that impacted me without us fully discussing the ramifications, I started feeling more and more uncomfortable. When one of those decisions created a timeline that meant I would have to give up my paying jobs to finish this project, without any financial support, I got that tight, anxious feeling in the pit of my stomach. All along, I had convinced myself that logic was certainly more trustworthy than a stomachache, but now I was confused.

During this time, an unlikely event brought me to my senses. I went on a hike with a friend and her puppies. At one point, the leash became twisted around the dogs' legs and ours. As we tried to free all twelve legs, I accidentally stepped on one of the dogs' paws. He immediately let out a squeal and we all jumped. "I'm so sorry," I told the puppy as I reached down to comfort him. Then, as if I had just peered into a giant mirror, I said aloud, "At least he yelps when he's stepped on. I don't say a thing!" And I began to cry. My submerged feelings had finally made it past the gatekeeper of my rational mind. The truth popped out of my mouth before I could stop it, emerging from some deep place of knowing that I had forgotten was there: I was feeling "stepped on." Yet I wasn't speaking up for myself, drawing boundaries, or taking firm action to bring the situation back into balance.

Being honest with myself after all this time was like letting myself see through the eyes of my soul. I saw that by ignoring my impulses, I was nowhere near honoring myself. I had done a great job conforming to someone else's outline for success, but was that mold really the right one for me? My anxious feelings had been trying to alert me to the answer, but I never got their message because I kept overruling them. I wasn't using my feelings to help me figure out what I wanted. Being honest with my-self also brought me face to face with the brutal truth that no one had forced me to continue along this track; it had been my choice. My choice was the real source of my unhappiness—and I could make a new choice.

MYTH:
Giving in to my feelings means I am weak.
Logic is more trustworthy than my feelings.

MAGIC:
My feelings serve a purpose and can
help guide me if I choose to listen to them.

After some deep soul-searching, I was at last able to articu-late for myself what the right kind of partnership for me would look like and then get support in spelling out my needs and con-cerns on paper. When I shared those with the person I had been working with, it turned out that we did not see eye to eye, and we could not reach an agreement that worked for both of us. Ultimately, I had to make a new choice—one that honored my heart's true desires. I chose to embrace the ending and free my-self from a situation that might have been right for someone else but was not right for me.

For someone like me, who has a hard time saying no for fear of letting others down, it was an extremely painful process, made all the more so because I had invested so much time and money into the endeavor. But how much was it worth to learn a lesson that would help me be true to myself for the rest of my life? In fact, this was a huge turning point for me, and I will always be grateful to my would-be partner and everyone in-volved in that situation. In a sense, each one volunteered to

[handwritten margin note, left side:] DOES NOT always MEAN you are wrong or somehow at fault or rejected. Just that it is not the situation you want.

[handwritten margin note, right side:] Tough to do But often necessary. Most people don't have the courage to do until the cost does perate or the situation becomes untenable.

appear in my life drama so I could learn key lessons—and they all played their roles to perfection. What an unforgettable way to learn that, yes, it is essential to listen to myself. Yes, ignoring my feelings and smothering my instincts will eventually make me terribly unhappy and get me tangled up in knots. And, no, the world will not end if I state my needs or say, "I'm sorry, but I can't." Acknowledging feelings and being honest, I discovered, go hand in hand. Both are prerequisites to honoring ourselves. Living without them keeps us totally in the dark.

GETTING AN ACCURATE INTERNAL READING

As if to reinforce all the lessons I was learning, during that difficult time I found myself talking to three others who reflected back to me the same themes. It seemed as if we all had the same homework and were comparing notes. We do often attract those who are working on the same issues we are. That is life's way of letting us know we aren't alone and of putting us in a position where we can help others by sharing what we've learned.

First, I ran into Bill, a friend I had worked with some years before. In the course of the conversation, I asked about his sister, Sharon. He told me that it had been the summer of her discontent. She was constantly complaining about her supervisor at the restaurant where she worked. "He's the worst manager," she would say. "He never fixes problems, so everyone else has to deal with one crisis after another. I've told him I want to work three days a week, but he's always scheduling me for extra days because of another crisis. It happens every single week."

Bill shook his head and said, "Sharon won't stand up for herself and she won't quit. I've told her again and again: Just say no. Draw your boundaries." It was clear that Sharon was very unhappy and that she felt used, but it was also clear that she wasn't doing anything to correct the situation. She was waiting for her boss to fix the problem when he was obviously incapable of doing so. In the meantime, she was getting more miserable and resentful. But who was really making her unhappy?

A few days later, a business associate announced to me that she was going to stop working with the woman she had hired to help her launch her new business. Originally, she thought that she couldn't be successful without the woman's expertise, but now, a year later, she realized that she could do the job better on her own. Then, not long after that conversation, I had lunch with an old friend I hadn't seen in years. She described a similar scenario. She was getting increasingly concerned because she was doing a large share of the work in a business partnership that was supposed to be based on equal effort. Even though my friend was adding most of the value, she wasn't being treated that way, personally or financially.

In each of those cases, including my own, I found myself asking: If she wasn't happy, why wasn't she doing something about it? Why wasn't she standing up for herself? Why did it take her so long to see what was happening?

One of the obstacles to turning the upside-down situations in our lives right-side up is that we rationalize that we have no other choice than to tolerate the intolerable. We don't get out of uncomfortable or toxic situations because we subconsciously fear that if we lose this job or that relationship, we'll never find anything better. Perhaps we don't believe that the universe does, in fact, want us to thrive and that it will support us when we let go and move on. Go deeper still and you will find that some of us tolerate downright dangerous situations because we don't believe that we deserve any better. We mistakenly believe that we need the support, praise, or love of the very person or thing that is causing us so much pain.

some people are incapable out of fear, personal experience and so on. The underlying problem is the Real issue

By harboring noxious beliefs like those, we numb ourselves to our real feelings and therefore don't get an accurate internal reading of the situation. So we stay stuck, even though our choice is, day by day, robbing us of the energy we need to accomplish what we really should be doing. This is not just an emotional dilemma. At its root, it is a spiritual malady whose symptoms stem from not honoring our true self, our inner spark—the part of us that remains when all else is peeled away. The fire that burns within us is the flame that nourishes us and drives us to fulfill our reason for being. Every time we ignore our feelings and refuse to end an unhealthy alliance because we believe we have no other choice, every time we are motivated to keep doing something because we believe we don't deserve any better, it's as if we are snuffing out a little more of that flame.

ACCEPTING WHAT IS

If you consistently shove your feelings into some dark corner where they can't be seen or heard, you are losing touch with one of your most valuable inner resources. I'm not advising, of course, that you give in to every urge or tantrum that washes over you as if you were catering to an unruly child who wants everything his way. Our feelings can indeed become distorted and drag us down when we are out of balance. As important as our feelings are, there is a paradox to be dealt with in the realm of our emotions: our feelings can guide us *and* they can also mislead us when we let them to get out of control (we'll get to that in a moment).

Rather than ignoring our feelings altogether or letting them sweep us off our feet, there is a middle way. We can learn to greet our feelings with open-hearted and compassionate acceptance. We can acknowledge our feelings without letting them

[handwritten marginal notes, left margin top:] SOME can not go this deep becoux they are afraid of what they will find or FACE it.

[handwritten marginal notes, left margin bottom:] FRUSTRATION ANGER Lack of CONTROL

rule us. Accepting an emotion doesn't mean we approve of what caused us to feel the way we do; it means that we accept what is. That is not our natural tendency. So often we resist the way things are, as if we could roll back the clock and change what has already taken place. Whether it's the e-mail we wish we hadn't sent, the words we regret having said, or the unexpected news that just arrived, the consequences of the past are already here. Folding our arms across our chests and saying no to what is standing right in front of us is simply unfruitful. That's what keeps us stuck, and brings us a lot of pain to boot.

Although it may seem paradoxical, by opening up to an uncomfortable experience, by accepting what is, we can move beyond it more easily. That's because we're no longer expending all the extra energy it takes to resist, attack, hide, or deny what has already come to pass. Instead, we can use our energy to create a solution. The moment you accept your feelings, you have taken a giant step toward honoring yourself. Leaving resistance behind frees you to take the practical action that is called for to help yourself and others. If you shut out your feelings, you've evicted both the messenger and the message.

Opening to "what is" with compassion and without judgment is a basic precept of mindfulness, a practice that can be found in many traditions around the world, including those of Taoists, Buddhists, Native Americans, and Christian comtemplatives, to name a few. Mindfulness is a way of being that encourages us to notice and accept thoughts and feelings rather than ignore or judge them. When we are mindful, we pay attention to what is happening in the present moment.

We all know what it's like to be hijacked by our feelings out of the present moment. Our feelings can suddenly ignite a fuse that sparks an explosion of painful memories from the past or fears about the future—and before we know it, we're time

[handwritten margin note: Sometimes you got Tired of Accepting "what is". I accept my feeling; I don't Like what caused me to Feel this way or get tired of experiencing it again & again.]

traveling again. We're lost in yet another story. The long and often tortuous storylines that zigzag through our heads masquerade as reality, but the past is long gone and the future is not yet here. Neither is reality. When our thoughts are anywhere else but here and now, we're merely chasing shadows.

How much of the time are you present and fully attentive to what is unfolding in the moment? How much of your day (or night) is taken up dwelling on a past event with regret or longing? How often are you lost in anxious thoughts about what might happen in the next half hour, the next week, or the next year? The sages tell us that we will never find peace by lamenting the past or second-guessing the future. The answers we seek are always in the now, but we can't recognize the gift that the now holds when we are running around somewhere else.

The Solution For Acceptance may be Now; but the Answer or Action may be in the Future.

KEEPING YOUR MIND STILL

It's not hard to understand why many of us have difficulty accepting "what is" and our feelings about it. When we see anything uncomfortable, painful, or stressful heading our way, our urge is to push it away, run away, or desperately fix it so that it will go away. Our mind jumps to conclusions without understanding what is actually happening, prompting our fight-or-flight response to take over. These reactions create a cascade of negative emotions that keep bouncing off of each other, breeding more agitation and more things to resist.

Where there is agitation, there can be no peace, no clarity, and no real solutions. Imagine trying to find something precious that you dropped at the bottom of a still, clear pond. If you frantically whirl around trying to find it, you will only stir up the dirt on the floor of the pond. The muddier the water gets, the less you can see. Yet when it comes to our own lives, that is often

Depends on how significant it was & or will be

what we do. Our impulse is to move faster and try harder, thinking that will bring us closer to our goal, but the opposite is true. In the waters of our own being, we must be still to find the treasure. You can't see what's real unless your mind is still.

———— 🌿 ————

MYTH:
*The faster I move and the harder I try,
the closer I'll come to finding what I seek.*

MAGIC:
When my mind is still, I can see what's real.

[handwritten note: NEVER MISTAKE ACTIVITY AS/FOR ACHIEVEMENT]

[handwritten note: NEVER MISTAKE EFFORT FOR SUCCESS]

Instead of trying to navigate in choppy waters, the mindfulness tradition opts for a more effective approach. To deal with turbulent feelings, it advises us to step out of the inner struggle and be compassionately present with what is taking place. Instead of resisting, it says, be receptive. Instead of getting submerged by the feeling, observe it. "Turn toward the experience with calm and focused attention," advises Dr. Jeffrey Brantley, founder and director of the Mindfulness-Based Stress Reduction Program at Duke University's Center for Integrative Medicine. "Recognize and accept that things are this way—now. Then work in practical ways to take care of yourself and to comfort yourself just as you would your own child or a friend who was in distress."[3]

Why is it so easy to get submerged in our thoughts and feelings or become paralyzed by them? For one, when we have intense feelings like anxiety or fear, we start to identify with them. When that happens, it's hard to separate what we are feeling from what is real. That's when you have to remind yourself, says Dr. Brantley, that the anxiety or panic you feel *are not you.* "They are actually only conditions that flow in and out of the

[handwritten note: AN AREA I NEED TO CONTROL BETTER]

present moment," he says, and achieving a calm, attentive state of mind makes it easier for us to let our thoughts and sensations arise "without becoming lost in them."[4]

One of the classic techniques to help us return to our calm center and be present with our experiences is mindful breathing—being still, focusing on the sensation of our breath as it moves in and out of the body, and gently bringing our attention back to that same point whenever our concentration strays. The world's spiritual traditions offer many other practices to help us slow down, focus, and clear distracting thoughts, everything from the centering prayer of the Christian contemplative tradition to some form of mindful movement, such as yoga, tai chi, labyrinth walking, or walking meditation, a form of mindfulness where you bring your full awareness to each component of every step you take. You can even practice mindful eating, as you slow down and fully experience the smells, tastes, and sensations with each bite you chew.

In reality, say the sages, any activity in life can be done in a way where we are fully aware of what we are experiencing and feeling in the present moment. And that is the whole point. The rituals and techniques are all ways to help us learn to live our lives with the eyes of our heart and soul wide open—seeing things as they are. With our eyes open and our mind still, we can respond rather than blindly react. Responding rather than reacting is an important distinction and a noble goal. Responding honors us because it pauses to listen for the message a feeling brings. Reacting doesn't bother to listen or honor; it stubbornly rushes headlong into the grooves of a well-worn reflex.

I'm very familiar with how getting lost in reactions rather than calmly responding to a situation can muddy the waters—and waste a lot of time too. If I'm not careful, my fall-back reflex—worry—can turn the most minor issue into an all-consuming goose chase. Once I enter the frantic zone, I lose my capacity to think clearly. To break that reaction, I have to remind myself to come back to myself by being still. I have to insert a quiet space that stops the momentum. I had another practice session in this the other night when I couldn't find the battery recharger for my camera after searching, literally, high and low. It wasn't an emergency that I find it, but it bothered me—a lot. Then it worried me—a lot. And then the emotions took on a life of their own. Looking back at the dialogue in my head and my knee-jerk "you've got to fix it now or else" reaction, I have to laugh, but it never seems funny at the time.

The recharger had been in my suitcase on a recent trip and I was sure that I had unpacked it when I got home. When I looked around and couldn't locate it in all the usual places, I started to worry. What if I had lost it? I rushed downstairs to the crawl space and, on my hands and knees, checked my suitcase again. When I saw that the recharger wasn't there, my anxiety carried me one more notch up on the worried scale and sucked me right out of the present moment. "I wonder what it will cost to replace that recharger? I bet the silly thing is way too expensive," I started to worry. "Maybe I left it in the hotel room. How stupid of me! My husband will *not* be happy when he finds out . . ."

Ten minutes later, I was still running around, searching under piles of clothes and whisking off the bed sheets, thinking that maybe the recharger fell inside the bed when I unpacked my luggage. I was mentally beating myself up, all over a tiny black battery recharger. Finally, I noticed that my heart was beating faster and I managed to stop myself. "This is not worth it," I said to myself. "I'm not honoring my time. I'm in that frantic pattern again and it's keeping me from finding what I'm looking for. It will either show up or I will buy a new one." I took a deep breath and resigned myself to "what is." Then a thought popped into my head: maybe my husband had packed the re-charger in *his* suitcase. I rushed over to his jumbo bag still sit-ting on the bedroom floor, flicked it open, and there it was, sitting on top of his socks. Creating a quiet, open space in my world had opened me to the answer that was there all along.

YOU ARE MORE THAN YOUR FEELINGS

It only took me ten minutes to stop the chain reaction that time (I'm getting better), and the stakes weren't so high. But as I work on staying mindful and in the moment, rather than giving way to a mindless, programmed reaction, I realize that the same prin-ciple applies when the anxiety or the worry goes deeper, because the pattern is the same. It's a habit.

The way we habitually respond to challenging situations may not disappear altogether, but we can learn to get better at noticing what is happening inside of us before our emotions get the upper hand—before their shock-and-awe campaign over-takes us. With that split second of awareness, you can stop, open a quiet space, and remind yourself: *I am not the worry or panic or fear I feel. That response is a habit, a pattern, but it's not me. The calm, abiding, knowing presence at the center is me. These thoughts and feelings—they are conditions that rise and fall. They are not stronger than I am and they are not permanent. The real me is.*

You can also remind yourself of the paradox we've been exploring here: *Even though my feelings are invaluable and I can learn from them, I am much more than what I feel.* You are more than your feelings because feelings aren't always based on truth. They can be triggered by false, judgmental beliefs you hold about yourself or others that make you judge, blame, or feel ashamed. You can learn to catch those false beliefs and misleading feelings before they take you hostage. You can grab them with the net of presence and tell yourself: *Feelings aren't always fact.* Then act on what's true and let what's not pass through.

As you practice observing your feelings rather than getting swallowed up by them, you'll become better at distinguishing valid feelings that call for concrete action from the ones that are just a blip on the screen. As for those blips, they are like clouds in the sky; they come and they go. We don't have to let them control us or define us. In reality, they don't. It's the stories we we spin around them that do.

———— ❧ ————

MYTH:
*My feelings will always
lead me in the right direction.*

MAGIC:
*My feelings aren't always based on truth.
I am more than my feelings, and I am
in control of what I focus on.*

———————

We all have a choice. We can stop resisting what is and be honest about our feelings without letting them take over. We can be compassionate with ourselves and learn from what we are feeling. We may not be in control of the thoughts or feelings that cycle through us, but we are in control of what we focus on. As the sages are fond of saying, you may not be able to change the emotion you are experiencing, but you can change your relationship to it. If you don't jump into the rollercoaster car of a runaway emotion as it whips by, your thoughts can't steal you away. By keeping still, you'll be able to stay in the present, right where you belong.

KEYS TO THE
BALANCING ACT

Facing Your Feelings

You receive invaluable feedback not only from your logical mind but also from your heart and your gut. When you don't take notice of your feelings or you resist them, you numb yourself to the important messages they are trying to bring. These seven questions can help you take an emotional inventory so you can learn more about your feelings, how you tend to deal with them, and whether you are staying true to yourself.

■ Do I ever tell myself that I must set aside how I feel because it's my job to grin and bear everything that comes my way?

■ Do I feel discomfort or doubt about situations in my life but keep trying to convince myself with logic or facts that my feelings aren't valid?

■ When I get anxious, do I push my feelings away? Do I drown out my feelings by staying perpetually busy or indulging in something that is unhealthy for me? What escape routes do I use to avoid facing my real feelings?

■ Do I take everything people dish out and later feel resentful or upset that I didn't stand up for myself?

■ Do I have a hard time expressing my feelings and speaking up for myself when others are making decisions that impact me or when I'm feeling dishonored, violated, or taken advantage of?

■ Do I blame others for situations in my life that are holding me back instead of using my feelings to figure out what I want and what action I should take to get unstuck?

■ Do I take time each day to tune into my feelings so that I am keeping the eyes of my soul wide open?

Check Your Vital Signs and Honor the Feedback

It's vital to take time out of your day to check your emotional vital signs—to listen to your instinctive feelings rather than push them away. Sit quietly where you can be uninterrupted. Relax and take some deep breaths. For a few moments, stay focused on the sensation of your breath as it moves in and out. Stay focused on this and nothing else. See yourself entering your heart and coming into harmony with its natural rhythm as you go through the following steps.

❶ Is there a situation in your life right now that is making you feeling uneasy or anxious? (You can pick a situation that came to mind as you were going through the previous inventory or choose another situation that you want to resolve.) Resist the temptation to judge yourself for feeling the way you do or to blame others for triggering those feelings. Feelings arise in all of us. They are part of life. Let them come naturally.

[handwritten note in right margin: NEED to Give Yourself a Break]

2 Compassionately acknowledge what you are feeling and say to your feelings: *I hear you. I am listening to your message. And I am staying in the present to take action.* If your thoughts start to pull you away from the present, chasing ghosts from the past or phantoms of the future—and that happens to all of us—gently affirm: *I honor myself by returning to the present, to what is in front of me now. I honor myself by staying in my heart.* By staying present and in your heart instead of jumping from one storyline to the next playing out in your head, you'll be able to respond wisely to what is happening. In your heart, you hold the creative solutions to any problem.

3 Listen to what your feelings tell you as you answer the following questions.

■ What am I feeling about the situation?

■ Where in my body do I feel the feelings?

■ How would I describe what it feels like?

■ If the feeling could talk, what would it say?

■ What belief, fear, or worry is driving this feeling? Is this belief or fear valid or am I jumping to conclusions?

■ What is this feeling asking me to do?

■ To follow through on what I have discovered and move on, what new choices can I make to help me feel at peace about this situation? (It may be that you need to take a specific action, or you may just need to acknowledge the emotion, let it go, and let it pass, like a cloud in the sky.)

CHAPTER 10

WHEN *the* WAY COMES *to an* END

When the way comes to an end, then change—
having changed, you pass through
—THE I CHING

Once you get in touch with your true feelings and take a stand for what you need, the events and people who come in and out of your life shift dramatically. New opportunities, better opportunities, always open up. Your inner flame becomes stronger and brighter.

Diane discovered how life-changing it could be to follow through on what her feelings were telling her when she was unexpectedly faced with an issue that challenged both her career and her character. She thought she had finally found a job that was in the right location and on the right career track. She was working directly with the owner of the company as his assistant. Then one day she discovered that her boss was dealing unethically with his clients. She knew this was wrong and hoped that something would come along to correct the situation so that she wouldn't have to rock the boat. But nothing changed, and Diane knew that she could not let the situation go unchallenged. When she finally mustered the courage to speak to her boss, he brushed aside her concerns. She told him that if he didn't stop his behavior within one week, she would quit. Seven days later, Diane found herself walking out the door holding a box of her belongings in her arms.

As she paused in the downstairs lobby of the office building to catch her breath, wondering what she would do now with no job, no severance, and no leads, an older, well-dressed gentleman stopped next to her. He was having some trouble opening his new briefcase. Diane instinctively offered to help and figured out the problem right away. "You're clever," the man said, thanking her. "If I'm so clever," she shot back without thinking, "then maybe you should hire me!" As it turned out, the man was looking for a good office manager. Diane was perfect for the job.

───────── ❧ ─────────

MYTH:
*If I let go of this relationship, job, or situation,
I may never get a better opportunity.*

MAGIC:
*When I say goodbye to a situation that isn't right for me,
I create an opening for a new gift to enter my life.*

───────────────

"He was so respectful, and that new job paid much more than the old one," she later told me. "I really didn't have to be worried at all about taking a stand for what I believed in or leaving that job." In fact, the universe was just waiting for her to make room in her life to receive that gift. Sometimes walking away is the right way to be walking. It creates an opening for life to work its magic.

When an ending comes, you may be tempted to greet it with regret, bitterness, or blame. Instead, face it with the certain knowledge that, for some reason, you need to turn off the road you are traveling on and take another route. Don't look back or hang your head as if you did something wrong or are being punished. Expect that your new adventure will, in its own time, reveal its reward and that this change is ultimately for your benefit. Make your new choices based on those truths and you will be honoring who you are and who you are to become.

THE PHOENIX IN US ALL

Why is it our natural reflex to blame ourselves or others when we are faced with endings? For one, we believe the myth that there is something wrong with endings—that they are unnatural. Perhaps what bothers us even more is that we are not in control of how and when those endings come. But how could we be? The only thing we are ever in control of is ourselves, not what whirls around us.

Benjamin Franklin once wrote that "in this world nothing is certain but death and taxes," but there is one more thing we can be certain of: things change. All things change. Endings are not exceptions to the rule; they are the rule. Each day comes to an end and then gives way to a new dawn. Each season transitions into the next. The new moon soon becomes a full moon, and vice versa. Our lives and the events that weave themselves through it are governed by the same universal cycle—birth, growth, maturity, decline, rest, and renewal once again.

The ancient Greek philosopher Heraclitus said, "The only constant is change." Tales and traditions the world around speak of this truth. Native Americans, for example, use the symbol of the circle to describe life's inevitable cycles of change and transformation. "The power of the world always works in circles," said Black Elk. "The life of a man is a circle. . ., and so it is in everything where power moves." The mystical Book of Revelation says, "I am Alpha and Omega, the beginning *and* the ending." Life's beginnings and endings are also reflected in the Hindu sacred trinity of Brahma, Vishnu, and Shiva, representing the Creator, Preserver, and Destroyer.

The Hindu tradition also portrays life's transformations through the iconography of Kali, goddess of life and death, transformation and dissolution. To understand the imagery evoked by the Hindu gods and goddesses, you have to realize that each one symbolizes and expresses a function of the divine. Their qualities and characteristics represent life processes that we, too, will experience. Kali is a paradoxical figure. Like the forces of change that visit us, she is at once ferocious and loving, fearsome and kind. She is portrayed with four arms, disheveled hair, and a necklace of skulls. Her two right hands confer maternal boons, representing the creative side of life with its new beginnings. On the other hand (in this case, her left ones), she wields a sword of knowledge and a severed head. These symbolize her ability to cut free humans from all that binds them to the unreal, bringing an end to their ignorance. Many endings in life spell the end of ignorance as we awaken to a truth we haven't seen before and decide it is time to move on.

Another profound and universal symbol of transformation comes to us in the ancient legend of the phoenix. That legend can be found, in one version or another, in many countries, including Egypt, Persia, Greece, China, and Ireland. It tells of an amazing bird who at a ripe old age builds a nest for itself, ignites it, and is consumed by the fire. From the ashes of its own ending, a new phoenix emerges.

———— 🌿 ————

MYTH:
If I try hard enough,
I can control what happens in my life.

[handwritten: ME - BuF I can't No Matter how hard I Try.]

MAGIC:
Endings are a natural part of life's cycles.
I honor myself by accepting them and
the transformations they bring.

————

All these traditions and many more are meant to remind us that we, too, are engaged in a continual dance of transformation as our outworn understandings, possessions, habits, relationships, and ways of being give way to new ones. When an ending comes knocking, you need not fear. Honor it and know that you, too, have the phoenix inside of you.

CLIMBING THE WALL

While modern society may place less emphasis on the milestones of our inner journeys, the imagery of endings reaching out to new beginnings can still be found today. Take, for instance, rites of passage like the Bar Mitzvah or Bat Mitzvah, which celebrate a coming of age, or our graduation ceremonies, which mark far more than the end of a level of schooling. Graduations not only signal the end of an era but also celebrate the beginning of a new one. That's why they are called "commencement" exercises.

When you experience an ending of any sort, think of it in the same way—as a commencement ceremony. Life is a schoolroom and, in many cases, our endings are actually graduations and promotions, although they may at first feel like just the opposite. Most of the time, endings come because we've learned one lesson and are ready for the next, or we've exhausted the possibilities that a situation has to offer and we need a change of scene to bring new opportunities. Endings are not only natural but necessary. When one appears in your life, you can be sure it has a purpose.

How do we know when it's time to celebrate an ending and move on? Think about how it works when a plant no longer has enough room to keep growing and becomes root-bound. When that's the case, the roots scramble for nourishment, literally climbing the walls of the pot. The plant begins to grow more slowly and doesn't yield all the flowers it could. To survive and thrive, it needs a bigger container filled with rich, new soil.

The same is true for us. When we don't have enough room to grow, we also start "climbing the walls." We slow down or become depressed. We don't feel vital and alive. If we don't take action ourselves to remedy this malaise, life will often do the honors for us. We'll suddenly find ourselves uprooted and transplanted without realizing why. If we're observant, though, we will come to see that the change is exactly what we needed. In fact, it saved us—it gave us new life.

It's not always easy to initiate our own changes, which is why life has a way of stepping in to do that job for us. I have a young friend who split up with her boyfriend of six years. Toward the end of their time together, he treated her badly and cheated on her. He was immature and she saw that they weren't on the same page emotionally or spiritually. While she knew that the break-up was good for her, for many months she had lingering doubts. One part of her thought that maybe they were supposed to be together, but another part instinctively knew that she had run out of room to grow in the relationship. She had become root-bound. It took her a long time to trust that her instincts were right and to realize that this young man's immature behavior was merely the catalyst life needed to engineer her breakout. In essence, the universe had fired him from the relationship and she had been promoted. It was as simple as that.

Like my friend, most of us have a hard time letting go and surrendering to endings. Maybe that is why life presents us with plenty of practice. Even the smallest of things can remind us to flow with change and embrace endings. That happened to me when my phone intermittently stopped working not too long ago. I refused to accept that the phone was breaking down and spent a lot of money on a special new battery. That didn't solve the problem, though, because the real problem was me. I didn't want to face the inevitable. As silly as it seems, I had become rather attached to my phone. I had programmed all my important phone numbers into it. I liked its white color. None of the new phones I saw looked as good to me as my old friend.

When it became apparent that I had to buy a new phone, I grumbled and expected the worst. Yet it turned out that the new one had several features that were very useful, and I soon wondered how I had ever done without them. I finally had to admit that having my phone break down wasn't an inconvenient nuisance or a gremlin's mean little trick. It had a purpose. And it taught me, yet again, that I can save myself a lot of time, energy, and money if I am just willing to let go sooner.

THE PAST IS ALWAYS PROLOGUE

Learning to accept endings has long been part of the human experience, as illustrated in this touching story from ancient India. When the only son of a young woman dies, she is so grief-stricken that she will not accept her loss. She carries her son, dead in her arms, to all her neighbors, begging for medicine to heal him of his sickness. Finally, one of her neighbors encourages her to speak with the Buddha. The desperate young woman finds him and once again asks for medicine to cure her son. He is moved by compassion for this poor woman, but he does not feed her platitudes. Instead, the Buddha says, "First, I must have a handful of mustard seed, and it must come from a house where no one has lost a child, husband, parent, or friend."

The young woman hurries from home to home, eagerly knocking on every door, but she finds no one who meets that requirement. In every home, someone has lost a loved one. Finally, late into the night, she sits down by the side of the road and watches the lights of the city flicker off one by one, like the lives of all those who pass on—like the life of her son. "How selfish I am to continue grieving like this," she says to herself. "Death comes to everyone. There is only one law, and that law is that all things are impermanent—all things change." With that realization, she is at last able to say a proper goodbye to her son and move on to the next phase in her life.

Although the endings and changes in our lives can, without a doubt, be painful, we make them more so when we label those changes as "bad," as "wrong," or as "failures" and then fiercely refuse to let go. The movie *You've Got Mail* is another good example of this. A small children's bookshop owned by the main character, Kathleen (played by Meg Ryan), is being forced out of business by a huge chain bookstore that opens nearby. It all seems so unfair. She clings to the way things are, even rallying public support for her cause, but to no avail. When her business finally fails and Kathleen must pack up and close her doors, she is unexpectedly handed a fantastic opportunity, one she would never have envisioned for herself. She is offered a job writing children's books. Now she can touch the lives of many more children than she could ever have done at her little shop. All the work she had put into running the bookstore was simply a prologue to this new venture. She had been in training for it all along. The ending turned out to be a promotion.

That story is all too typical of what we tend do when faced with unexpected endings, whether it's a broken-down phone, a deteriorating relationship, or a pending layoff. When an ending is in the wings getting ready to walk on stage, we may develop a desperate urge to hold on to what we are comfortable with. We frantically want to fix a situation and hang on to it, when our inner self is asking us to transcend it altogether. We only prolong our sorrow and pain when we refuse to accept that the endings are really choreographed by our own souls for our own good.

Taking the plunge into the unknown can be scary, but once we embrace endings and face forward rather than continually looking backwards, the doors of transformation open wide. Joseph Campbell, the renowned American scholar of mythology, made that point when he described "a bit of advice given to a young Native American at the time of his initiation: 'As you go the way of life, you will see a great chasm. Jump. It is not as wide as you think.' "[1]

CHAPTER 11

PUT DOWN *the* LOAD *and* FLY

*"He abused me, he beat me, he defeated me,
he robbed me"—in those who harbor such
thoughts hatred will never cease.*
              —THE DHAMMAPADA

In the circle of giving and receiving that is your life, one of the most powerful forms of giving will always be giving the benefit of the doubt. Giving the benefit of the doubt means setting aside your preconceptions. It means checking your snap judgments, grudges, and resentments at the door so you can truly see what is in front of you for what it is, unsullied by your prejudices—your pre-judgments.

A favorite wisdom story of mine, from the Hasidic tradition, illustrates what can happen when we let go of the limited thinking of our judgmental habits. A rabbi would sometimes retreat to a hut in the woods to spend time alone. One day while the rabbi was there, the abbot of a nearby monastery knocked on the door and asked to speak with him. The abbot explained that he was troubled because only five monks now lived at the monastery, all over seventy years old. He was afraid that soon there would be no one to carry on their traditions and wondered if the rabbi could give him some advice. The rabbi admitted that he, too, was seeing dwindling numbers in his synagogue. "I have no advice for you," he said, "but I can tell you one thing—one of the monks at your monastery is the Messiah."

The abbot shared this surprising news with the other monks. It seemed a long shot that any of them could really be a Messiah, but they couldn't help but ponder the rabbi's words. Of course they all had idiosyncrasies, but what if what the rabbi said were true? With that thought in mind, the monks began to overlook one another's irksome habits and to look more closely at each other's good qualities. Just as importantly, each monk began to appreciate his own virtues rather than focus on his faults. In short, as the weeks passed the monks became less critical of one another and of themselves. They began to honor each other and honor themselves. The seed the rabbi had planted was taking root.

Every summer the people in the nearby towns would come to picnic on the grounds of the monastery. This year they noticed how much reverence and warmth the holy brothers had for one another and their visitors. The monks were extremely kind and respectful. They exuded peacefulness and joy. Some of the young men living in the area began asking the abbot if they could join the order and share the monks' special way of life. Those young monks, in turn, attracted others. Soon the monastery was not only full of life, but it had also become a shining example of love in action to all the surrounding communities. By giving up petty judgments and giving each other the benefit of the doubt, the five elderly monks put an end to the limiting thinking that had been holding them back. As they focused on their positive qualities, those positives blossomed and bore fruit far beyond their lives.

This story brings up a key question: Is the purpose of life, or even of spirituality, to enumerate our faults and eradicate all the ways our personalities don't seem to conform to the rules? Or does the inner art of giving and receiving, the very art of life itself, ask us to appreciate the best in ourselves and others, knowing that when we do, those qualities will grow stronger and brighter?

[handwritten margin note: DAMN good Question]

MYTH:
The world becomes a better place when I focus on eradicating my faults and helping others do the same.

MAGIC:
What I focus on, I energize. Whatever I appreciate in myself or others—grows stronger and flourishes.

The power of appreciation cannot be overstated. Appreciation is the supreme motivator and magnifier of good. Mother Teresa once observed that "if you judge people, you have no time to love them." When we appreciate rather than criticize, we move out of the mental, judgmental mode and operate from the heart—and whatever the heart nurtures always grows abundantly. While it's important to self-correct and to guide those under our care, we all make more progress more quickly when we are appreciated and praised. How often do you take a moment out of your day to move into your heart and tell your friends, family, or co-workers, in specific terms, how their words, actions, or talents have personally helped you?

[handwritten margin note: ME!]

[handwritten margin note: Not Enough. Sometimes saying thanks needs more explanation]

The notion that what we appreciate grows stronger is not just another cliché. How we see and treat others has deep implications for us. When we judge others and refuse, ever so subtly, to give them the benefit of the doubt, we are restricting what we ourselves can receive. As spirituality author Elizabeth Clare Prophet so aptly put it, "We limit ourselves each time we limit another." The reason for this is simple. If your heart isn't big enough to contain the brightest image of others, despite how they have behaved before, you certainly won't be able to envision what you yourself can become. By expanding your heart to give the benefit of the doubt to others, you create more room for yourself to grow too.

WHEN WE DON'T FORGIVE

What if we've given someone the benefit of the doubt and that person hurts us or others again and again? How can we put an end to resentment, open our hearts, and keep giving? It's not easy. Even after we have said goodbye and are long gone from the scene, the memory of those hurts can linger.

There is only one real reason we don't forgive more easily, and that is that we harbor misconceptions about what forgiveness is and what happens when we forgive. The picture many of us have in our heads is that forgiveness is for weaklings. We think forgiving is giving in to a bully who has no business pushing us around. We may also believe that by forgiving, we are condoning the perpetrator's harmful behavior and giving that person the green light to keep acting that way. Those are no more than myths.

Forgiveness does not require that you approve of another's outrageous behavior or foolishly subject yourself to it again. You can forgive and still take steps to protect yourself. You can forgive and still be clear about what you will not accept in your life from now on. In addition, the act of forgiveness does not

People should not need to question certain things. you should have no Doubt in their mind.

Some Time People hide behind a mask And say Things like "That's Justme" excuse any of us from being accountable for our transgressions. Forgiveness does not wipe out the fact that an action someone took was despicable.

Rabbi Harold Kushner explained this to a resentful woman in his congregation who was struggling to support three children after her husband walked out on them. When she asked Rabbi Kushner how she could possibly forgive this man, he said, "I'm not asking you to forgive him because what he did was acceptable. It wasn't. . . . I'm asking you to forgive because he doesn't deserve the power to live in your head and turn you into a bitter, angry woman." Then he told her that by holding on to resentment she was not hurting her husband; she was hurting herself. Forgiveness, writes Rabbi Kushner, is not about what we do for another person. "Forgiving happens inside us," he contends. It means saying, "I refuse to give you the power to define me as a victim."[1]

———— 🌿 ————

MYTH:
By forgiving others, I am condoning their behavior and releasing them from accountability.

MAGIC:
By forgiving, I do not condone harmful acts or excuse people from being accountable for their actions. By forgiving, I free myself.

————

By forgiving and giving someone the benefit of the doubt, you may very well free him or her to have a second chance. What matters most, though, is the paradoxical truth that forgiving others *frees you*. Oddly enough, we tend to believe that by refusing to forgive others, we are cutting them out of our lives, thereby ending our connection with them. But continuing to hold a

[handwritten marginal note:] I wish I could do this better. People you have hurt you not only By Sins of Commission — what thy have done — But also by Sins of Omission — what thy have not said or done.

grudge—emphasis on the word *hold*—is no ending at all. By harboring bitterness, resentment, or even the desire for revenge, we remain mentally and emotionally invested in what happened. That only keeps us in relationship with—connected with—the very people we want to say goodbye to.

Attention is energy. Whenever you place your attention on another person or thing, you are creating a flow of energy between the two of you. It doesn't matter if your thoughts are loving or if they are filled with irritation and anger. In either case, you are creating an energy bond that is fed by your attention. The mystic Saint Germain described the tremendous power of our thoughts when he said, "Attention is the key; for where man's attention goes, there goes his energy, and he himself can only follow."[2] When you understand that energy equation, it's easy to see that you automatically tie yourself to anyone you continue to hate, resent, or be angry with. You may think that rancor is the right response when you want to distance yourself from others, but at energetic levels your bitterness binds you to them. It strengthens the connection.

Another way of looking at what happens when we don't forgive is that our resentment literally saps our vital energy. It divides our attention so that we no longer have 100 percent of our energy available to pour into the areas of our lives that need our attention. We create a situation that is like trying to water our garden with a hose, only to discover that just a tiny trickle is coming through because the hose has large holes in it. Until we repair the leaks, we will only get a fraction of the water that could be coming through. Although we may fool ourselves into thinking that withholding forgiveness gives us a measure of control, in reality whatever we allow to siphon off our valuable energy and attention controls us. When we do not forgive, it is we who suffer. Perhaps you've heard this saying that puts it even more strongly: not forgiving someone is like drinking poison—and expecting the other person to die.

MYTH:
By refusing to forgive, I am in control.

MAGIC:
What I do not forgive controls me.

A graphic portrayal of what happens when we hold on to our anger comes from the movie *Return of the Jedi* in the Star Wars series. During the climactic scene, the evil emperor and Darth Vader are face to face with Luke Skywalker. The emperor has been patiently waiting for the opportunity to turn Luke to the Dark Side, just as he succeeded in doing to Darth Vader many years before. As the emperor and Luke confront each other, the old man goads Luke as he spits out these words: "The hate is swelling in you now. Take your Jedi weapon. Use it. . . . Strike me down with it."

Then the emperor sums up exactly what anger and nonforgiveness do to us as he says to Luke, "Give in to your anger. With each passing moment, you make yourself more my servant." The emperor knew that the more we hate, the more we surrender ourselves to the object of our hatred. Fortunately, Luke controls himself before it is too late. By putting his attention back on his real self and on love, he not only saves himself but is also able to bring Darth Vader back to the Light Side.

Lest you think that all this sounds a bit too intangible and that the benefits of forgiveness are metaphysical mumbo jumbo, know that a burgeoning field of research is proving otherwise. Studies have shown that holding on to blame, hostility, and anger can harm us in very tangible ways. One study, for instance, showed that unforgiving thoughts prompted significantly higher heart rates and blood pressure changes, whereas forgiving thoughts were accompanied by lower physiological stress responses. In research with people who suffered from chronic low back pain, those who were able to forgive had lower levels of pain and less anger and depression than those who had not forgiven. People taking part in experiments with "forgiveness interventions," where they learned how to forgive relationship partners, exhibited increased levels of hope, greater self-esteem, and lower anxiety and depression. In another study, women who had forgiven the fathers of their children for transgressions had less symptoms of anxiety and depression as well as a greater sense of self-acceptance and purpose in life than unforgiving women.[3] These and other experiments show that the harm we inflict on ourselves when we don't forgive is not only an emotional burden but a physical one too.

STOPPING THE MOMENTUM

As you begin to sort through the misconceptions that may be keeping you from unleashing the power of forgiveness, you may find a few more myths hanging out in the cobwebs. Have you ever entertained the notion that you must be sure that justice has been done before you can move on? Have you ever felt that you must understand why something happened in order to be at peace about it?

"Why did this happen? Why me? Why now?" we ask ourselves. You may learn the answers to those questions. Perhaps you'll uncover the lesson an incident was meant to teach you or a hidden blessing it held. Perhaps it released you from an unhealthy relationship, made you stronger, or prepared you to help others deal with the same issue. Perhaps what felt like a betrayal even saved you from a situation that would have turned into a colossal calamity down the road. Maybe the wound you sustained even helped the person who hurt you finally see the folly of his or her ways. Still, the underlying reasons and lessons may not be obvious until much later. In fact, you may never understand the why behind an incident. Does that mean you should wait to forgive and to be at peace?

A wonderful story from the life of the Buddha goes to the heart of that question. A monk who was one of the Buddha's students once bitterly complained that his teacher's discourses never addressed the deepest metaphysical questions, such as whether the world is finite or infinite, eternal or not eternal. The monk was extremely unhappy about this and said that if the Buddha did not give him those answers, he would return to his old way of life. The Buddha replied that when we wait for answers to those kinds of questions, we are like a man who is shot with a poisoned arrow but tells the doctor when he arrives, "I will not allow this deadly arrow to be taken out until I know the name of the man who wounded me, his height, the color of his skin, what town he comes from, the kind of bow he used, what the bow string was made of, and what kind of feathers made up the shaft." The wounded man will die before he receives the answers to his questions, and neither his survival nor his healing depends on them.

On what, then, does our healing depend? We all get hit by slings and arrows of outrageous fortune from time to time. Is it more important to know "Why did this happen? Who was responsible? And how can I pay them back?" Or do we heal more quickly and live more fully by taking out the poisoned arrow, honoring the ending, and setting ourselves free?

When we harm another, each of us certainly has to answer
for our actions and be accountable, and that is why we have a
system of justice, whether in the home, at school, or in court.
Yet, the sages tell us, we are subject to an even higher law, a universal one that automatically operates in everyone's life: the law
of the circle. If we propagate anger and hatred, that is what we
will reap—sometime, somewhere. If we extend love and forgiveness, that is what will return to us—sometime, somewhere.
The world's traditions are clear on this point. Whether they describe it as karma, the law of cause and effect, "what you sow,
you shall reap," or simply "what goes around comes around,"
the principle is the same.

We may not be privy to how that law of the circle will play
out in other people's lives. How and when justice is dispensed is
not necessarily within our power. What is within our power is
getting our own lives back on track and putting an end to the
cycle of hatred and vengeance within our own backyard. Not
one of us wants hatred or violence in our lives; and yet when we
don't forgive, we are the ones who keep it alive. We complain
about the growing violence and hatred on the planet, yet we
play our roles in adding to that momentum whenever we choose
to be unforgiving ourselves or to return a harm done to us with
compound interest. Our own bitterness feeds the beast. *Which Wolf?*

Even in the most difficult and heartrending situations, we
have the power to say, "The momentum stops here." The popular Buddhist classic known as the Dhammapada presents that
poignant truth in these verses: " 'He abused me, he beat me, he
defeated me, he robbed me'—in those who harbor such thoughts
hatred will never cease. 'He abused me, he beat me, he defeated
me, he robbed me'—in those who do not harbor such thoughts
hatred will cease. For hatred never ceases by hatred but by love

alone is healed. This is an ancient and eternal law. . . . We all will one day perish; those who know this, their quarrels cease at once."

CREATING A NEW STORY

"He hurt me, she betrayed me, he cheated me"—those are all snapshots of what may have happened at one moment in time. By clinging to that story, by retelling it and reliving it, we accept what happened during one segment of our lives as the whole story of our lives. It is essential, of course, to remember grave injustices, whether they have been done to individuals, peoples, or entire nations, so that we can prevent such outrages from occurring again. As the philosopher George Santayana wrote, "Those who cannot remember the past are condemned to repeat it." Nevertheless, the story of what happened to you, or what you did to someone else at one time, does not have to become *the* story of your life. You have the power to create a new story. What happened does not have to close down your heart and shut down your capacity to give and receive—unless you insist on letting it.

What someone else says or does can only continue to weigh you down if you carry around the memories of those actions like a perpetual sack of good-for-nothing stones strapped to your back. How freeing to just put down the load and move on. How much faster and farther you can travel. Without the burden, you can even fly.

Ultimately, forgiveness is another way of honoring yourself. By forgiving, you are affirming that you are greater than what others think of you or do to you. You are also affirming, as challenging as it might be, that those who commit harmful acts are

What if a loved one continually does this? Do Actions speak louder than words? In my mind—yes. But that is not the point :-

potentially greater than their actions. They may not know that yet; but by compassionately forgiving, you are helping them to see that that is the case.

———— 🌿 ————

MYTH:
If I forgive, I am shortchanging and dishonoring myself.

MAGIC:
By forgiving, I am honoring myself. I am affirming that I am greater than what others think of me or do to me.

———————

The opportunity to forgive, then, is just that—a stunning opportunity *for you*. Will you allow another's immature behavior to define you now and forever? Will you let the incident forever define the person who hurt you? Will you decide to keep carrying the load, or will you put down your burden, honor the ending, and let yourself fly?

[handwritten margin note: Hard to do especially when you grow up hearing Certain Things you loved ones Treat you a certain way.]

FINDING THE WELL IN THE DESERT

Apart from all the myths we've examined so far in this chapter, there can be another dynamic at the heart of our suffering— we blame ourselves. This gets back to the syndrome we looked at in chapter 8—hanging on to the false belief that if something painful happens to us, it's always because we have done something wrong.

Like children who blame themselves when their parents argue, separate, or abandon them, we might lay all the blame at our own feet in order to make sense of what happened. "Why did I let this happen?" we say. "What's wrong with me? How could I have let this go on for so long?" Perhaps you could have done something to prevent what happened; but if you are to honor yourself, you must see the situation as part of your own personal learning curve in the advancing classrooms of your life. Even the most aching and barren times do indeed hold some lesson or gift for us. Rather than feeling that you must blame yourself or others to make it through hard times, try looking for the gift instead. Like the little prince in Antoine de Saint-Exupéry's beautiful fable, *The Little Prince*, you can say to yourself, "What makes the desert beautiful is that somewhere it hides a well."

It has helped me immensely to search for that well in the dry spots of my life. When I catch the old refrain "What is wrong with me?" running through my head, I try to ask, "What did I just learn about myself and what did I learn about the way life works?" Those have been much more fruitful questions. The answers have taken many forms: "I can look inside of myself for guidance instead of assuming that someone else knows best." "Remember to think before you say yes." "I can find a better way to do this that won't hurt others." "I make the best decisions when I trust my feelings." "Next time, I will stop fixating on the past, extract the lesson, and move on more quickly." While the lessons have varied over the years, in every case they point me back to the same resounding theme: *What can I do to honor myself so I can give my gifts to others?* And they remind me, with stunning consistency, that to do that I must leave blame and regret behind. By putting down the load, I am free to soar.

KEYS TO THE
BALANCING ACT

Releasing Regrets

Is there an ending in your life that you've never fully accepted because you still blame yourself or others for what happened? Regrets are a sign that some part of you is still walking around in the past and that you are operating with less than 100 percent of your energy in the present. Releasing the situation and reclaiming all your energy is a step-by-step process, and it can be challenging. Yet trying to move forward with the rest of your life while you are chained to the deadweight of the past will be far more difficult. The following tools can help you start to honor the endings in your life so that you can greet the new beginnings they always bring. You can also use these tools whenever a new situation arises that makes you feel hurt, resentful, or angry.

■ **Uncover hidden regrets.** Sometimes we aren't consciously aware that we still harbor regrets that burden us. You can use questions like these to identify hidden regrets that may be stealing your energy: *What incidents from the past still come to mind from time to time and make me feel angry, resentful, or unhappy? Do I feel like a victim? Have I allowed this event to define the whole story of my life when I still have the rest of my life to live? Do I secretly blame myself for allowing or contributing to someone else's harmful behavior?*

■ **Depersonalize.** Studies show that empathy as well as depersonalizing what happened can help us forgive more quickly. Empathy doesn't mean that you approve of someone's hurtful behavior, but putting yourself in another person's shoes can help you become more objective and therefore deal more effectively with the issue at hand. Ask yourself: *Even though I don't approve of what that person did to me, can I see what may have caused him or her to do it? Have I ever been in a comparable situation myself and either reacted in a similar way or been tempted to?*

■ **Look for the lesson.** We have all experienced a painful ending that later turned out to be a blessing. Perhaps it freed you to pursue something better, taught you an invaluable life skill, or led to your life's work. No matter how unpleasant an incident, there is something you can gain from it. Ask yourself: *What insight, information, or invaluable lesson am I supposed to gain from the experience? What did I learn about myself or about the others involved? How will I apply what I learned to the rest of my life?*

■ **Take action so you can move on.** If you regret something you did in the past, you don't have to let those events constantly float through your mind and burden you. Instead, take action to bring resolution. Find the person you hurt and apologize, even if the event took place years ago. Replace something that was lost or destroyed as a result of your actions. Assign yourself a serious task that will at least begin to make up for what happened (do volunteer work, help an elderly neighbor with chores, teach a child to read, work in a soup kitchen). Being proactive rather than passively letting regrets plague you will help you come to closure and move on.

■ **Create your own ritual of release.** Doing something physical to honor an ending can help you release it once and for all. There are many ways you can do this. One ritual I've found helpful over the years is to write a letter to God (using whatever name you prefer to address the creative Spirit of the universe). You can pour out your feelings on paper and ask for help in letting go and finding peace. You can say that you are turning over the situation to God as well as releasing your attachment to everyone involved. Then burn the letter in a safe place with a prayer of surrender on your lips. You can also ask that what you wrote be carried as an inner message to the people who were part of the situation. As the fire envelopes the paper, see and feel the memories and burdens being consumed by the flames. Another effective ritual is to hold an object in your hand, like a special stone or shell, and visualize your feelings about the incident being transferred into it. Then, as you give an affirmation or prayer of your choosing, cast the object into the ocean or off the side of a mountain. Whatever you choose to do, create a ritual of release that has meaning for you—one that will help you honor the ending and free yourself.

PART FOUR

CELEBRATE YOURSELF *and*
HONOR YOUR OWN VOICE

Insist on yourself; never imitate. . . .
Do that which is assigned to you, and you
cannot hope too much or dare too much.

—Ralph Waldo Emerson

Honoring our own voices and choices is not easy in a world that presents us with more voices and choices than ever. To do so, we must resist the tide that would pull us along with the crowd. And to do that, we must learn to celebrate who we are. While life provides us with mentors and role models to guide us along the way, in the end we must depart from all mentors and models. Their path may not be our path, and their final destination may not be our own. The sages say that our job is not to become our teachers, parents, friends, or advisors, but to become ourselves. Often the hardest part of that equation is learning to trust the process, savor the moments, and fall back in love with who we are.

CHAPTER 12

YOUR INBORN NOTE

Everything on the earth has a purpose, every disease an herb to cure it, and every person a mission.
—MOURNING DOVE (CHRISTINE QUINTASKET)

"There is nothing new under the sun." Myth or magic?

A Zen student once said to his teacher, "Brilliancy of the Buddha illuminates the whole world." Even before he had finished the phrase, his teacher said, "You are reciting a poem by someone else, aren't you?" "Yes," replied the student. "Then," said his teacher, "you are side-tracked."

We cannot help but become sidetracked when we choose not to express our own voices and when we become comfortable with consistency and conformity—those two enemies of the soul. In his powerful work "Self-Reliance," Ralph Waldo Emerson extols the opposite virtues: *inconsistency* and *nonconformity*. "Why should you keep your head over your shoulder?" he asks. "A foolish consistency is the hobgoblin of little minds. . . . With consistency a great soul has simply nothing to do. He may as well concern himself with his shadow on the wall." Once you begin to play with nonconformity and inconsistency—pushing yourself to experience the unusual and giving yourself permission to change an opinion you held ten minutes ago—slowly but surely your own voice will emerge.

You do have a unique voice, and you do have something unique to say. In this respect, you and I are a bit like penguins, those hearty creatures who seem to be conformists, all in their identical black-and-white tuxedos. Yet they are anything but identical in ways that matter the most. Each penguin is born with a distinct "voice" that sets him or her apart. This individuality comes into play as penguin parents raise their newborn. After the mother lays her egg and transfers it to the father, she takes off on a long sojourn to the sea to feed herself so she can return to nourish her newborn. Meanwhile, the father's job is to keep the egg warm in temperatures that can approach -80°F. Once the egg hatches, he protects the chick as they await the return of its mother some two months later.

In the coming months, the parents shuttle back and forth from the sea to eat and then feed their young. Each time they return from their arduous treks, the penguins' icy breeding ground resembles a vast sea of black-and-white look-alikes. How do the fattened mothers and fathers know which of the penguins is their mate and which of the tiny, furry babies is their own? The penguins have a unique call, or vocalization, as well as a built-in recognition system that allows them to identify each other and to answer the call of their young. Like our penguin friends, each and every one of us possesses a unique "voice" that can be recognized by those who nurture us and by those we are destined to nurture.

SOMEONE NEEDS TO HEAR YOU

To say that you, like a snowflake (or a penguin), are entirely unique may sound like just another platitude. Yet have you ever considered the implication of this cosmic artistry? If you have been endowed with something unique, you can bet there is good reason for it—someone needs to receive your gift. If you don't make your voice heard, those who are hungry for what you have to offer won't recognize you. That's how nature works and that's how we work. Your job is to honor your voice and share it with those who need to hear it, no matter what those who don't want to hear it have to say.

Perhaps you've hesitated to do that because you think "I'm no one special." Maybe you don't believe that you possess a gift, talent, or ability worth honoring. That is a myth. Every one of us has a gift to give. If you don't know what yours is, that doesn't mean you don't have one; it just means you haven't discovered it yet.

——— 🦢 ———

MYTH:
I'm no one special.

MAGIC:
I have a special gift that someone needs to
receive and a unique voice that someone needs to hear.

———

You may have bought into the myth that "I'm no one special" because you have accepted another untruth—the myth that you must have a high IQ, a well-honed professional skill, or an acclaimed accomplishment to qualify as "gifted." Some of us subconsciously believe that our ability to give, and therefore our right to receive, is defined by the letters that follow our name. Yet the labels that others give us, whether positive or negative, are never the essence of who we are.

Define who you are. Don't allow others to do it. You will never be satisfied.

A beautiful tribute to a hard-working peasant in Henrik Ibsen's play *Peer Gynt* illustrates that point. In a eulogy by the peasant's grave, a priest speaks of the silent suffering and disdain the peasant bore throughout his life because the townspeople believed that as a young man he had chopped off his own finger to escape military service. The peasant was not wealthy or wise, says the priest, and "his voice was weak, his bearing unmanly." Yet this man's heart was good and his life was one of supreme service to his family, though he was later forgotten by his three sons grown into prosperous gentleman.

Praising this humble man for being true to himself, the priest says: "No patriot was he. Both for church and state a fruitless tree. But there, on the upland ridge, in the small circle where he saw his calling, there he was great, because he was himself. His inborn note rang true unto the end."[1] When you sound your true note within your circle of influence, however faint it appears to be, you make your greatest contribution to the world.

MYTH:
*To make a real contribution to society, I must have
letters after my name or an acclaimed career or craft.*

MAGIC:
*The labels people give me do not determine my true worth.
I make my greatest contribution to life when I am myself.*

What is your inborn note? I once met a woman in the waiting room of a doctor's office, where we struck up a conversation. She was so cheerful that I couldn't help but remark on that wonderful feature of her personality. When I did, her big smile got even bigger as she told me that she thought that cheerful quality defined her life's purpose. She leaned towards me and whispered excitedly, "I believe it's my job to uplift everyone around me. I show up at work in the morning and I try to make everyone who steps through the door of the office a little brighter." I was impressed with her candor. She wasn't being egotistical or prideful. She simply knew who she was and why she was here. She had found her own voice.

That woman knew that she didn't need a set of letters behind her name to be of value. I have attended gatherings, though, where some of the women plainly diminished themselves because they felt they were "just mothers," with no fancy career description or list of abbreviations after their names. Yet those women are the ones who exude both sweetness and power. They are sensitive and strong. Although they don't see it, it's clear that they are making a huge impact on the world because of *who they are*. Who they are inevitably influences the children they lovingly raise, who will in turn influence and set the example for many others in an ever-widening sphere of influence.

Who we *are* is always more important than the label that describes what we *do*. The sixteenth-century Spanish mystic Teresa of Avila expressed that truth when she wrote that God "does not care so much for the importance of our works as for the love with which they are done."[2] Another, more recent Teresa, Mother Teresa, is famous for saying that the most important opportunities are not to do "great things" but to do "small things with great love."

In today's world, however, we tend to define who we are not by the "small things" through which we express our inborn note, but by what kind of job we hold or by our list of credentials (or lack of them). We also measure our value by the number of items we've managed to check off our to-do lists. When we are at a party or are meeting someone new, don't we habitually ask, "What do you *do*?" Your career or job may very well

[handwritten margin note:] And By the SAME TOKEN SomeThings PeoPle CAN NOT See the difference. I wANT To know who you are Not what you do.

[handwritten bottom note:] A Self Defining Process Because we Fail To See or Accept who we are And look at thing To define us.

be the vehicle you use to express your reason for being, the stage on which you share your gifts. Or it may not. In either case, what you do is never the totality of who you are.

No matter what we "do," one day we will all have to answer the following question, which, like a Zen koan, forces us to go beyond the images we have formed of ourselves and contemplate what really creates meaning in our lives: *When you have nothing left to do, who are you?*

NOT SOMEDAY, BUT NOW

We can spend so much time doing, planning to do, and forging the path toward what we want to be someday that we forget about "being." We forget to appreciate who we are now, in the process of becoming who we will be next. It's hard to appreciate who we are right now if we look at now as somewhere in the middle of a race to the next finish line—the line that we glimpse from a distance but that never seems to get any closer no matter how far or fast we go. Our culture tends to measure success in terms of that illusive finish line. Many of today's self-help gurus also advocate that we set our sights on the future, focusing on who we want to become in order to attract what we are visualizing into our lives.

The sages, whose wisdom has outlasted the ups and downs and changing fads of the times, point us in another direction. They tell us that holding in mind the vision of our goals is only half the story. It's just one piece of another paradox. For the steps we take along the way are as important, if not more important, than the big picture. Your choices and actions in each moment are the threads that weave the tapestry that, in the end, will tell the story of your life.

Looking for life's meaning in the pieces that make up the whole was advocated by Dr. Viktor Frankl, a psychiatrist who survived the horrors of the Nazi death camps and went on to develop his own landmark approach to psychiatry. Think of your life as a movie consisting of thousands upon thousands of pictures, each one carrying a meaning, Frankl explains in his seminal work, *Man's Search for Meaning*. In order to understand the whole film, you first have to take into account each of those individual pictures. Frankl encourages us to deal with our lives in the same way—to focus on the meaning that is "inherent and dormant in all the single situations" we face. The meaning of life not only differs from person to person but also "from day to day and from hour to hour," he says. "What matters, therefore, is not the meaning of life in general but rather the specific meaning of a person's life at a given moment."[3]

While the little pieces that make up your life may seem insignificant, in the grand scheme of things they are of greatest consequence. To put it another way, you could say that the answer to the question "What is the meaning of my life?" will ultimately be seen through the answer to another question: "What choice am I making right now?"

That view of life is liberating, especially for those of us who find ourselves perpetually sprinting toward a finish line. It encourages us to refocus our attention on the opportunities right in front of us. It eases the anxiety that can grip us when we fixate on a future that seems scary or unattainable, on a goal we're not sure we're ready to take on. Greeting one moment at a time frees us to live fully as we dive into each moment and share the best that we can be in that moment. Life, you could say, is a series of choices you make in the now, and therefore sounding your inborn note is not something you will do *someday* when you have enough schooling, enough skills, enough money, the right kind of job, or a big enough audience. Giving your gifts is something you do *now*, moment by moment.

THE BIG PICTURE AND THE PRESENT MOMENT

Our modern way of life, with its communications that fly across the globe in an instant, keeps us scurrying so fast from one appointment or activity to the next that it takes a concerted effort to stay anchored in the now. Focusing on the now does not, of course, mean we should never make plans or set long-range goals. That is important too. Yet if we are forever looking into the far-off future, we can easily miss what each moment has to offer us—and what we have to offer in each moment.

MYTH:
*Keeping my eye on my long-range goals
is the most important thing I can do.*

MAGIC:
*The present moment is as important as the big picture.
What I choose to do and be in this moment is what
gives my life meaning and momentum.*

In order to slow down and savor the moment, we have to be willing to trust. We have to trust that the opportunities set before us in the moment are like strokes of a master artist; each stroke contributes to the masterpiece, even if we don't yet see its purpose as part of the whole. As we do our parts right now, more of the picture will reveal itself.

Appreciating the beauty of the now also requires us to stop rushing past the moments as we race toward the goal line. To sit still. To appreciate the *quality* of the moment rather than the *quantity* of sensations we can cram into it. To borrow an analogy from the twentieth-century writer and Trappist monk Thomas Merton, some of us scurry through life as if we were visiting a museum with a guidebook in hand, racing to see all the highlights before our visit comes to an end. When we do that, we come out less alive than when we went in, says Merton, because we've "looked at everything and seen nothing."[4]

To give a concrete example, if we fix our gaze only on a goal in the distance, like completing a certain project or getting promoted at work, we might become oblivious to the people standing right in front of us who need our love. We might run over anything that's in the way of our reaching our goal. How satisfying is it to finally reach the finish line, only to look back and see a path strewn with the wounded we have tackled, shoved aside, or abandoned altogether? How successful are we when we collapse after years of unrelenting strain and then don't have the strength to enjoy what we have worked so hard to create?

That kind of living is "half-living." It's like putting on eyeglasses that have very strong corrective lenses for long-distance vision. We can see far-away objects perfectly, but everything up close is a blur. Of course, the opposite syndrome is also "half-living"—being so nearsighted that we focus only on what's happening right now, right in front of us, without giving a thought to planning for the future or considering the consequences of our actions.

Focusing on the big picture of our long-range goals *and* staying alert to what's happening right now is a paradox that invites us to dance to a different rhythm as we move through our days. It prompts us to ask new kinds of questions, questions like these: *What can I give now* (not just what do I plan on accomplishing someday)? *In this moment, what do I have the opportunity to*

In the left margin, handwritten: *I Am Giving up this Lifestyle. It doesn't SATISFY me Soul!!!*

learn, give, or receive (rather than how can I influence or use what's happening to benefit me so I can get ahead)? *What can I experience and savor in this moment* (rather than how many phone calls, projects, or errands can I check off my to-do list today)? <u>*What kind of a person do I want to be*</u> (not just what do I want to do)?

Like all paradoxes, working toward long-range goals *and* keeping in touch with the present moment are not mutually exclusive. One doesn't detract from the other. Instead, they work together synergistically to help us express our inborn note to the fullest. They are two parts of the whole that when finely tuned can create the magic of full-hearted living. That's because when we take time to honor ourselves by opening to the present moment, it's actually easier to meet our long-range goals.

Take this story of two spiritual seekers who embarked on a trek to visit their teacher at his home high on a mountaintop in the Himalayas. Their tale is not so different from ours as we make the trek up our own mountains in life. As the two climbed the steep mountain path, one of them kept stopping to enjoy the view and take in the beauty of the wild flowers growing along the way. This annoyed his companion, who was intent on reaching their destination as quickly as possible. At last, they arrived at the mountaintop and sat at the feet of their teacher, imbibing his wise words. Later that day, they began the long trek back to their home. Once they had returned, they sat down to rest next to the fire and began to recollect the wisdom their teacher had shared with them. It turned out that the one who had paused to relish the flowers and scenery along the way could remember much of the teacher's valuable instruction, while the one who had expended so much perspiration and energy to reach the mountaintop could not. Which one had really reached the goal more quickly?

CHAPTER 13

WALK *in* YOUR OWN SHOES *at* YOUR OWN PACE

I am absolutely unique, I am I, I am incomparable. The whole weight of the universe cannot crush out this individuality of mine.
—RABINDRANATH TAGORE

The Sufi teacher Nasrudin stopped by a shop one day and asked the owner if he had any leather. "Yes," the shopkeeper said. "How about nails?" Nasrudin added. "Yes," the shopkeeper replied. "And do you have dye?" queried the sage yet again. A third time, the man answered yes. "Then why," asked Nasrudin, "don't you create a pair of boots for yourself?"

The writings of the Sufis, the mystics of Islam, feature the wise master Nasrudin playing the part of the fool (as many teachers will) to reflect back to us what should be obvious but is not. In this case, Nasrudin is trying to awaken us to an important truth: You already have the inner equipment you need to walk far and wide on your own life path. You just have to put the pieces together in a way that is uniquely suited to you. No one can create your life or express your creative spirit for you.

Life is never a one-size-fits-all formula. It's not intended to be mechanical, nor you to be passive. You are meant to create your own formula for self-discovery and self-expression. For the answers, and even the questions themselves, are never the same for any two of us.

Ultimately, life beckons us to accept the leading role in our lives. Yet it's so easy to settle into the mode of observer and allow someone else to tell us how to act, eat, dress, buy, worship, and even be happy. The deeply entrenched sense of dependence on something outside of us to steer our course is one of the major dilemmas not just of our time but of all time. The luminaries of the ages have worked hard to stir us from this complacency. Do not blindly follow what you hear, they advise, but test it out. Apply it to your own life. Experiment. Your life is your laboratory. There is no replacement for direct experience.

the control Agents. Church + Govt. T.V. and society.

Thousands of years ago, for example, the Buddha reminded his students that their individual progress as well as their community's success did not depend on him. As he was dying, he told them: "Be ye lamps unto yourselves. . . . Look not for refuge to anyone beside yourselves." That is not solely an Eastern concept; it is a universal one.

One early Christian text, probably written in the late second century, echoes the Buddha's words when it advises: "Light the light within you. Do not extinguish it! . . . Knock on yourself as upon a door and walk upon yourself as on a straight road. For if you walk on the road, it is impossible for you to go astray."[1] And before that, Jesus gave the message to look within for the answers when he said that the kingdom of God is inside of you *and* outside of you.[2] "If you bring forth what is within you," another text quotes him as saying, "what you have will save you."[3]

Likewise, the renowned Muslim philosopher Abu Hamid al-Ghazali taught the importance of relying on oneself when he wrote, "Nothing is nearer to you than yourself, and if you know not yourself, how can you know anything else?"[4] More recently, Mohandas Gandhi said, quite simply, "The only tyrant I accept in this world is the 'still small voice' within." These and many more teachings from the world's sages point to the truth that your happiness as well as your spiritual progress are the result of choices you make for yourself, not choices others make for you.

MYTH:
*I can make the same choices and take
the same steps that have worked for others.*

MAGIC:
*I value my mentors, but I also ask
my own questions, seek my own answers,
and shape my own life.*

You may be thinking that self-reliance is all well and good, but don't we also need the help of those who can take us under their wings and show us the ropes—isn't that what the sages are supposed to do? That is true, and that is precisely the paradox at play here. We do need teachers and supporters, who come in many forms and guises (as we explored, in part, in chapter 4). As the Sufi mystic Rumi bluntly observed, "Whoever travels without a guide needs two hundred years for a two-day journey."

Whether you are an aspiring ballerina, financial wizard, first-time parent, or spiritual seeker, you need a guide who has been there before and can lead the way—*and* you must also rely on yourself. Seek the guidance of the wise ones, the sages urge, but realize that their role is to lead you back to your own inner sage. Your mentors are meant to inspire you to look into your heart, discover your strengths, and become your own version of great. Like Nasrudin, the best teachers will point to the leather, nails, and dye in your workshop. They will show you the work that needs to be done. But they will expect you to make your own boots. The teacher is the starting point; you must do the rest.

HONOR YOUR OWN STYLE

If you are to develop and give your gifts, you must honor who *you* are and celebrate your own voice. Depending solely on others is like taking a long walk in borrowed shoes. If you've ever hiked in someone else's shoes or in new shoes that don't fit quite right, you know what I mean. If the shoes are even a bit too big or too small, they can be very uncomfortable. If you walk long enough under those conditions, you'll get blisters. Eventually the pain becomes so bad that you can't go on. That's what happens to you when you force yourself into a mold that isn't your own. The remedy: *walk at your own pace and in your own shoes.*

Admittedly, I've been somewhat recalcitrant on this point, and therefore life has generously given me many lessons to teach me to trust myself and to be myself. One dramatic lesson came in an equally dramatic landscape. I was hiking in the beautiful Teton Range near Jackson Hole, Wyoming, with two friends. Both are taller than I am and they walked briskly, covering more ground more quickly than I could. At the time, I didn't think about the fact that nature had endowed both of these women with long, strapping legs that could scramble up the steep path like mountain goats. Instead, I blamed myself for not being able to match their pace. "Something is wrong with me," I thought to myself. "I must really be out of shape. If I just push a little harder, I can keep up." So that's what I did. I pushed, and then pushed some more. My strategy worked, but halfway through the hike, the consequences set in. I pulled a muscle in my hip without realizing it. The ache I felt at the time was tolerable until we started the long descent down the mountain. At that point, every step I took was painful. It hurt so much that I couldn't even tolerate the weight of my small backpack, which my friends had to carry for me. On top of it, I got an upset stomach and felt sick the entire way home.

I don't remember much about the sights, smells, or sounds of that day. I don't remember much of anything except the pain. I forfeited my ability to enjoy the trek by struggling to keep up with someone else. But I did learn an invaluable lesson: *if you don't walk at your own pace, you will only end up hurting yourself.* Over the years, when I've been tempted to take an action that doesn't honor my own style, speed, or destination, I've thought back to that experience. In a few cases, I wish I had recalled that episode much sooner. It might have saved me the anguish of another long practice session in self-reliance.

WHOSE ROLE WILL YOU PLAY?

When you are walking in someone else's shoes, at someone else's pace, or on someone else's path, you are not honoring your authentic self. And when you are not yourself, you cannot be at peace. That can be a hard-earned lesson for those of us who have found ourselves living the lives our parents, spouses, boyfriends, girlfriends, role models, bosses, or business partners say we should live, only to wake up one day wondering why we are miserable. Walking on your own path and being "at peace" does not mean that you won't experience challenges. You will. Like a wise and demanding coach, life will always push you to stretch beyond your current limits so that you can increase your ability to give and to receive. When you commit to living and giving in your own way, though, the challenges that greet you will be part of your own inner blueprint and not another's.

The ancient Bhagavad Gita (literally "Song of God") explores the mandate for authentic living in its famous exchange between the sage Krishna and the warrior prince Arjuna. Their dialogue takes place on a battlefield, where Arjuna and his brothers are poised to reclaim their rightful ancestral kingdom from usurpers. Paradoxically, Krishna offers to aid both sides in the battle; he lends his armies to Arjuna's enemies while he serves as Arjuna's personal charioteer, protector, and advisor.

As the battle is about to begin, Arjuna surveys the opposing side. He sees among the enemy's warriors his own kinsman and old friends. Although he knows that his cause is just, the thought of what he must do makes him heartsick. Overcome by despair and grief, he drops his bow and sinks to the floor of his chariot. There, in the middle of the battlefield, positioned between the two waiting armies, Krishna eloquently explains to Arjuna that he was born to play the role of warrior. It is his calling, and he must fight.

While the battle in the Bhagavad Gita may have been an actual event, it is also symbolic of the struggle we all face—the battle to rule our own internal kingdom, to take charge of our own life, and to live true to our own inner nature. Krishna tells Arjuna that the real battlefield is within. It is doubt and selfish desire that we must slay. Do what you are born to do on the field of life, he says, not out of greed, hatred, egotism, or the desire for personal gain. Do it out of love. Do it unselfishly, without attachment, and for the good of all, and then you will

<u>attain peace.</u> Arjuna commands the sullen warrior: "Do thy duty, even if it be humble [or imperfect], rather than another's, even if it be great. To die in one's duty is life: to live in another's is death."[5]

Those are strong words—words that were meant to resound through the centuries and send a clear message to all who would hear them. For over two thousand years, the Bhagavad Gita has inspired millions who have seen in Arjuna's challenges their own and who have heard in the Gita the call to be their real selves. In one way or another, we will all have to answer the questions that Krishna put to Arjuna: Will I embrace my own calling or will I take an easier path? Will I choose my work solely because it will bring me recognition and reward or will I choose the work that will help me share the gifts I was born to give? In the face of doubt and fear, will I opt out of the struggle or will I summon the courage to act?

RESISTING THE PRESSURE OF THE "MOB"

Living as your authentic self always comes with an added assignment—the task of resisting the pressure to conform to the crowd. Ralph Waldo Emerson was as great a champion of that cause as you will ever find. "Trust thyself" is his cry. "Trust thyself: every heart vibrates to that iron string," he wrote. He despised the trend of bending to the will of the masses. "Now we are a mob," he lamented, adding that it is hard to stay true to yourself "because you will always find those who think they know what is your duty better than you know it." Emerson pointed out that the challenge is not simply to be yourself when you are by yourself—that is easy. The truly great person is the one who "in the midst of the crowd" can keep his or her independence "with perfect sweetness."[6]

The only way to survive the momentum of the "mob" is to think for yourself and to be honest about what you think. When we are faced with "the intruding rabble" or even family or friends who want us to conform to their beliefs or expectations, Emerson suggests a humble but frank affirmation of self-honoring truth: "Henceforward I am the truth's. . . . I appeal from your customs. I must be myself." In the end, he says, "nothing can bring you peace but yourself."

The strong pull to conform to what is happening around us is carried to the extreme by Woody Allen in one of his most artistic films, *Zelig*. To conform is literally "to form together," to shape into the same form as something else, and Zelig is a man who has the uncanny ability to do just that. If he is with a group of overweight people, he automatically becomes overweight. If he is with a group of doctors, he becomes a doctor. He is so desperate to fit in that, like a chameleon, he transforms into the type of person he is with. Emerson, I think, would appreciate the parody.

Today, with the massive reach of the media, we are faced with more opinions about who we should be, how we should act, and what we should think than ever before. The crowd is so much bigger, so much brighter. But the crowd will not support your freedom to shine in your own way. It will never support who you are. It will try every trick possible to reshape who you are in its own colorless image. One of its strategies is to lure you away from your inner priorities by getting you to focus on something entirely outside of yourself that seems to be more interesting and more exciting.

Our celebrity culture with its fixation on the "stars" makes that kind of diversionary tactic easy. Just look at the huge popularity of television series like *American Idol* and similar programs around the world. Don't get me wrong. Relaxing with some good entertainment is essential, and it's healthy to applaud another's gifts and greatness. Looking up to role models can give us the impetus and inspiration to come up higher ourselves. However, when we become obsessed with the comings and goings of others, we are the ones who lose because we are giving our valuable energy and attention to a pet idol instead of investing those precious resources in ourselves. Besides, you cannot sing your own song if you are always humming someone else's tune.

IFS AND IDOLS

An idol, by definition, is a false god or something we blindly or excessively adore. We usually think of an idol as a person, but we can adopt many kinds of idols. An idol can be anything outside of you—whether a person, group, organization, possession, or belief system—that you have assigned the power and responsibility to make you happy. By that definition, our idols can take the shape of the magic bullet, the quick fix, or "the magic if," as I call it. *If only* I would get that promotion. *If only* I lived where the weather was always nice. *If only* my children or parents or partner would stop misbehaving. *If only* I could have some peace and quiet. *If only* my boss would appreciate my work. *If only* this health problem would go away. *If only* a wonderful man or woman would walk into my life. *If only* I would win the lottery . . . *then* my life would be perfect and I could fulfill my dreams.

If you are waiting for someone to appear or something to happen before you take your next step, you most likely have an idol; and your belief in that idol is holding you back. Why? Simply because, as one Zen saying puts it, "If you look for the truth outside yourself, it gets farther and farther away."

Few of us are without our idols and our "magic ifs." They are so embedded in our way of life that we may not realize we have them—and so many of them. There have been times in my life when I have procrastinated as I've waited for someone or something to create the ideal situation for me to get on with giving my gifts. I learned that it doesn't work that way. We have to find a way to give our gifts no matter what the people in our lives do or do not do. If we find it impossible to be true to ourselves within our current circumstances or relationships, then it's time for us to change those circumstances or relationships. The only real power our idols have is the power we give them, and that is our power. When we reclaim that power, we free our inner spirit.

MYTH:
*Someone or something outside of me can
rescue me and make my life perfect.*

MAGIC:
*When I let go of my idols, I free myself
to express my creative inner spirit.*

Idols, in whatever form they come, are a dangerous distraction. The more we believe that they have superior powers, the less we believe in our own innate powers. This famous Zen koan gets to the heart of the issue: "If you meet the Buddha on the road, kill him."

That expression is paradoxical, shocking, and mind-bending all at once. That's because a koan is meant to shatter our conventional ways of thinking. In essence, this one is telling us: Let go of your idols. Do not blindly accept something as truth because it came out of the mouth of someone you look up to or even revere. Discard the idea that a particular person, perspective, or institution will automatically know what's best for you. Don't let your attachment to what's outside of you keep you from reaching what's inside of you. Respect what others have to offer, but find the truth for yourself. Experience the answer for yourself. Honor yourself.

KEYS TO THE
BALANCING ACT

Honoring Your Own Voice

You have a special gift that you are meant to share with others, a unique voice that someone needs to hear. Take a moment and reflect on the following questions to get in touch with how you think about your gifts and whether you are honoring your own voice. As you answer these questions, remember that you share your gifts not only through what you do but also through what you are.

■ **Do I appreciate my unique gifts?** What special qualities or talents do you possess that you can use to help others? Is it your joy, compassion, or patience? Your attention to detail or ability to bring people together to get a job done? Your talent as a musician, healer, teacher, cook, parent, or coach? Is it the way you support others to express their best talents? (Hint: If you don't know what makes you unique, ask yourself: What do people say they appreciate about me? Ask a close friend, partner, or co-worker to candidly share with you what qualities they appreciate most in you.)

■ **Do I celebrate my strong points?** Most of us are in the habit of concentrating on our shortcomings rather than applauding our positive qualities. To help you celebrate who you are—who you *really* are—save all the cards, e-mails, and letters people have sent to thank you or express what they value or love about you. Save other mementos that help you bring to mind your strong points, your accomplishments, and the joy you have given others. Put them in a special box or folder. Someone I know calls this her "feel good file." When you're beset, upset, or have lost sight of your smile for a while, pull out that collection. Read what's inside to remind yourself that the drama or trauma that happens around you is not who you are.

■ Am I waiting for something outside of me to make things "perfect"? We all wish that something or someone would sweep into our lives and, like a bejeweled fairy godmother, wave a magic wand and make everything perfect. The sages consistently teach that our own thoughts, actions, and choices—not those of a fairy godmother, an idol, or even a respected mentor—create the meaning in our lives. Take a piece of paper and fill in the blank in this statement with as many things as you can think of. "*If only_____, I could move forward and be happy.*" After you have done that, for each item on your list ask yourself, "*What specific step can I take to create the change I am waiting for?*" When you answer that question, don't reject any ideas that come to you. Don't limit yourself. Get creative and you will be surprised how much control you have over your life—if you are willing to take it.

■ What is on my to-be list? What we focus on becomes a reality. That's why we create weekly and daily to-do lists. They help us stay focused. As important as what you *do* is what you *are.* To remind yourself to focus on the kind of person you want to be, create a to-be list for the week right alongside your normal to-do list. Ask yourself: *What do I want to be like this week? What qualities will I consciously work on expressing*

[handwritten marginalia: No one can make you happy but you. Some people see no distinction. No distinction. Depends on what mood they are in or what they have already done.]

(such as patience, honesty, appreciation, trust, self-esteem, being fully present and in the moment when I'm with my loved ones, et cetera)? During the week, challenge yourself to express the qualities on your to-be list of intentions.

■ **Who are you?** You are more than your to-do list. You are more than what you say, what job you hold, or what you own or do not own. Take some quiet time for yourself and write down the answer to this question: *When you have nothing left to do, who are you?*

SOME People iDenTIFY SO STRong
with this part of LIFE they don't even
Realize they can be MORE. SOME hide here
And SOME BASE their ENTIRE mental
outlook / health on the STATUS of their
LIST, Not SelF, FRIENDS, Family
CHILDREN OR SPOUSE. They
I denTIFy so strongly with
their "to-do's" "Need to's" and
"hAVE-To's" they SACRIFICE the
MEANINGFul Relationships on this
or their thinking about it.
or what Else Needs to be done.

CHAPTER 14

EVER MORE MAGNIFICENT

Journey from self to Self
and find the mine of gold.
　　　　　　　—JELALUDDIN RUMI

Creating your own life takes courage, patience, and persistence. At times, it can feel as if you're walking from one shore of a river to another against a strong current that will sweep you off your feet if you stop pushing for even a moment. That unrelenting current, whether it's the current of conformity or resistance to your dreams, isn't the real danger, though. The real danger is doubt. Doubt is what causes us to pause midstream. Doubt is what allows the current to sweep us off our feet. We question ourselves, and we question whether the universe will support us in being ourselves. When we give doubt free rein, we become susceptible to the insidious propaganda that says we must move with the current of the crowd because, it slyly whispers, "you are not good enough to do anything else."

A lot of people never take the 1st stupid some around.

I think For some it is And this is what tly want.

It is difficult to celebrate your true voice when you hear voices like that rumbling around in your head, reciting the litany of your past "mistakes" as evidence that you should give up. Those voices may seem so familiar that you automatically believe them. After all, you may have heard them, in some cases, as far back as you can remember. But the voice that judges, belittles, or limits is never the voice of your true self. It is the voice of the false self, that inner trickster and saboteur who tries to paralyze you by playing both sides of the question. On the one hand, it tells you that you aren't capable of much because you're imperfect. On the other hand, it criticizes you because you haven't accomplished more!

As a result of listening to that two-faced harpy, it can seem more appropriate to feel guilty about what we have not accomplished than to celebrate what we have. We label our learning experiences, the situations where we grow the most, as miserable failures and a waste of time. Afraid of making another mistake, we hesitate to try anything new. All this masks the real truth that there can be no waste of time when we are learning—and we are *always* learning.

We've all heard the words of pundits like Albert Einstein, who said, "Anyone who has never made a mistake has never tried anything new," or James Joyce, who said that "a man of genius makes no mistakes" because his errors are "the portals of discovery." Intellectually, we know that mistakes are good and that they are the best way to gain life experience. That's what all the latest business books, self-help gurus, and success seminars teach, isn't it? Nevertheless, our conditioning and our habits, reinforced by our environment and the people in it, may signal otherwise.

How often have you been patted on the back with the words "Atta boy/atta girl! What a great mistake that was! Let's celebrate!" Most of the time, the reactions to our learning experiences, anything from being rejected or laughed at to being spanked or fired, amplify the notion that getting love and approval depends on how perfect we are at any given moment. When we are immersed in that kind of feedback, there *is* one thing we do learn to do perfectly—criticize ourselves. We learn to be good judgers and we do it constantly. We can rattle off all the ways we aren't good enough rather than recount what we have learned in the process of living and loving. We become like the person Archbishop Fulton Sheen once joked about who went to the doctor complaining of a headache.

"Do you feel a distressing pain in the forehead?" the doctor asked him.

"Yes," said the patient.

"And a rather throbbing pain in the back of the head?"

"Yes."

"And piercing pains here at the side?"

"Yes!"

"Ah!" the doctor explained, "your halo is on too tight."

THE MYSTERIOUS, MOVING TARGET OF PERFECTION

How do we know if we are afflicted by the "not good enough" syndrome? Life coach Brook Montagna helped me diagnose this syndrome in myself when, during a process of self-discovery, she asked me to list all the ways I saw myself as "good enough" and then list all the ways I saw myself as "not good enough." I made two columns on a sheet of paper and immediately skipped to the "not good enough" column. That was easy to figure out, and I filled it up in a snap. As for the "good enough" column—well, that was another story. I hesitantly squeaked out a few entries but gave up after several minutes. When it came time to

[handwritten margin note:] Easy to live if perfect and Not so much if Not. Put in the effort if Not. Easier to point out get upset if Not. Most don't, they focus on our Faults on

report back in and Brook saw the results, she paused and then gently asked, "Did it ever occur to you that you are already good enough—just as you are?" Frankly, it hadn't.

Her comment caused me to do some deep self-reflection. I wondered what kind of internal measure I was using to decide what part of me was "good enough" or "not good enough." And good enough for what? Brook pointed out to me that what I had listed in my "not good enough" column were actually traits. We all have personality traits or habits that bother us, and others, but they are not reasons to label ourselves as woefully inadequate, undeserving, and at our core "not good enough."

When I asked Brook how many of the people she works with have the same difficulty I did with that exercise, she said that most people do. Not long after that, a conversation I had at dinner with friends reinforced that unfortunate fact. One of my friends was describing how her twenty-something niece had shocked her parents by telling them that when she was growing up she had never felt good enough—that phrase again! The girl's parents were understandably upset to hear this. When my friend finished her story, though, I asked, "Did *you* feel good enough when you were growing up?" "Well, no," she admitted. In fact, only one lucky person around the table that night, among both men and women, said that she had not suffered from that awful feeling of inadequacy when she was growing up. From time to time, I have asked that question to others, and it's a rare person who escaped with a high level of self-esteem.

While our teenage years can be challenging, I don't believe for a minute that feeling inadequate is simply part of the natural passage through self-conscious adolescence, a phase that disappears with time. Patterns like that are ingrained in us long before we become teenagers, and they can last long after. Although we might be adroit at hiding it from others and ourselves, that feeling of being "not good enough" can still be alive and kicking in the subterranean world that rules so many of our thoughts and actions.

The real problem with this scenario is that if you classify yourself as "not good enough," when can you consider yourself a success? When can you allow yourself to be happy? When can you start enjoying who you are and what your life has to offer right now? When is it okay to stop judging yourself against that mysterious, moving target of perfection?

At the root of this conundrum is a misunderstanding. Many of us have been duped into believing that everything we do must measure up to the stiff standard of human perfection. The luminaries of both ancient and modern times take a much more heart-centered view. Life is indeed a progression, the sages tell us. We are meant to be constantly growing and transcending our previous know-how at physical, mental, emotional, and spiritual levels. As students in the classroom of life, we naturally get the most out of this process when we strive for excellence rather than remain passive. Yet the sages also emphasize that the goal of our lessons is not to live up to some unapproachable ideal of mechanical perfection. The goal is to discover yourself—your true self—and to express more of your true self each day as you open your heart and expand your capacity to give your gifts.

We all yearn to express our real selves and share our gifts completely. As Rabindranath Tagore wrote, "this longing for the perfect expression of his self is more deeply inherent in man than his hunger and thirst for bodily sustenance, his lust for wealth and distinction."[1] Thomas Merton directs us to the same truth, but from a Christian perspective. "For me," he writes, "to be a saint means to be myself. . . . We are at liberty to be real, or to be unreal. We may be true or false, the choice is ours."[2] We don't make that choice once. We make it every day, sometimes many times a day. As we go about our daily activities, we can choose to let our real self express itself through us, or we can acquiesce to the fearful and self-critical self that pretends to have our best interests at heart but only reinforces the musts and shoulds that keep us rendering the verdict of "not good enough."

VOTING FOR YOURSELF

If you continually choose the measuring stick of the false self over the real self, you will be chasing the elusive target of perfection forever, never happy, never at peace. The antidote to that stressful way of living is to embrace both sides of the paradox. Acknowledge that you do not have to be humanly perfect to be happy or to be worthy of love *and* that there will always be room for you to grow and improve. You are good enough *and* you are always getting better. When the critical voices come sneaking up on you, summon the courage to say: *"No, I am not humanly perfect. Who is? Human perfection isn't the issue. Being my true self and being my best self is. Today I will strive to do my best as the steppingstone to what I am becoming next. I am voting for myself."*

How do you vote for yourself? You do it each time you command the voice of judgment that says "that was stupid" to get a grip on reality and stop being so dramatic. You do it each time you assert your right to learn from your missteps without calling them failures. You do it whenever you choose not to automatically blame yourself when something seems to go wrong. You vote for yourself when you make the choice to be with people who are positive and encouraging. And you do it each time you admit with a smile that, like everyone, you are a work in progress.

When the young Vincent Van Gogh's mentor, Mauve, became upset with him, Van Gogh artfully defended himself as just such a work in progress. In a letter Van Gogh wrote to his brother, he said, "Mauve takes it amiss that I said, 'I am an artist,' which I won't take back, because it's self-evident that what that word implies is looking for something all the time without ever finding it in full. It is the very opposite of saying, 'I know all about it, I've already found it.' As far as I am concerned, the word means 'I am looking, I am hunting for it, I am deeply involved.' "

That is a refreshing point of view. It underscores that we don't have to be "perfect" to pursue our chosen quests. What's far more important is to be "deeply involved" in the process of living—to affirm that "who I am and what I have to offer is always evolving." It is counterproductive to judge yourself while you are in that process. And you will always be in that process. You *are* the process.

〰

MYTH:
*Getting love and approval
depends on how perfect I am.*

MAGIC:
*Human perfection is not the goal.
Learning to express more of my true self is.*

[handwritten annotation: Depends on who loves you. Why. Depends on you Act Ego]

We are all the artists of our own lives—painting, repainting, and sometimes deciding to start over on an entirely new canvas. We are all hunting for the right medium, technique, and splash of colors that will capture what we are trying to create at this point in our lives. From the time you are born, you are working on your masterpiece. You are improving your skills. A young painter doesn't start out being a master artist any more than we pop out of the womb possessing all the skills of a mature adult.

Do we label it a mistake when a toddler sways from side to side and falls on her fanny again and again as part of the process of learning how to stand on her own two feet? Does that indefatigable toddler or her parents view her clumsy attempts as a mistake? Of course not. So why should we get upset with ourselves when we are in the midst of mastering certain life skills? Why should we judge ourselves when we are learning, ever more skillfully, how to open our hearts, share our gifts, and receive the gifts that others have for us? Why should we get discouraged when we are still honing the inner art of giving and receiving?

Even the most clever geniuses among us consider themselves to be lifelong learners. A reporter is once said to have asked American inventor Thomas Edison how it felt to fail thousands of times before succeeding in inventing the light bulb. Edison patented more than a thousand inventions in his lifetime, and his answer to that question shows why he was so successful. "I have not failed," Emerson replied. "I've just found ten thousand ways that won't work."

The eccentric Howard Hughes, in his own billionaire way, provides another example of exulting in the process of learning. During his movie-making career, Hughes spent millions of dollars filming and refilming the epic *Hell's Angels*, a film about two brothers who join the British Royal Air Force and volunteer for a dangerous mission in World War I. It was by far the most expensive movie of his time. Hughes was obsessed with making it better, take after take after take. Yet he never looked at the process as a defeat or a mistake. He called it a learning experience. To those who questioned whether it was really sensible to whittle away his fortune on a movie, he would say, "You think I'm just wasting time, but I'm learning a lot about making movies." In the end, *Hell's Angels* became a spectacular hit and was nominated for an Academy Award for best cinematography. Hughes went on to produce many more films. Some turned out to be flops, but others live on as film-making classics.

"*I am learning a lot.*" That's a good comeback to the voices inside and out that will doggedly try to drown out your true voice with their judgment. "*I am learning a lot about who I am.*"

THE GOLD AND THE MUD

It would take an entire book to dissect where the entrenched idea that we are not innately good enough came from and how it has managed to stick to so many of us like duck tape to paper. We would have to explore everything from how and when the idea of "original sin" first entered the scene (in fact, centuries after Christianity was born) to what's behind the cultural stereotypes of success that are relentlessly pounded into us through every imaginable medium. What is more to the point here is focusing on strategies to combat the condemning voices and champion the truth. Those strategies all start with affirming what the wise ones teach—that you are at heart a magnificent being in the process of becoming ever more magnificent.

———— 🦅 ————

MYTH:
I am not good enough.

MAGIC:
*I am a magnificent being in the process
of becoming ever more magnificent.*

That empowering truth is a thread that runs through all the world's great traditions. If you study what the founders and mystics of those traditions taught, you will find that they high-light our innate worth rather than reinforce our weakness. They celebrate our inner fire rather than focus on the threat of hell fire. They say that what matters most is not how well we toe the party line or follow the rules, but whether we honor and ex-press the magnificent power and potential inside of us. I love the way an early Christian text called the Gospel of Truth poeti-cally puts it: "Say, then, from the heart, that you are the perfect day, and in you dwells the light that does not fail."[3]

The sages describe the process of getting in touch with your true power as an awakening. Wake up from your dream, they say, the illusion of who you think you are or have been told you are, and see yourself as you really are. Go beyond the outer trap-pings and search for the inner essence. The mystics describe our inner essence in a variety of ways, adapted to their unique times and cultures. Christian mystics speak of the inner man or inner Christ while Quakers refer to the Inner Light. Our inner essence is known as the Atman to Hindus, the Tao to Taoists, and the Buddha nature to Buddhists. Others call it the divine spark, the real self, the higher self, or simply the Self.

No matter what terminology they use, the mystics say that our real self is one with the divine. Although it may appear to be playing hide and seek because we forget that it is there, our real self is always with us. One Buddhist text, for example, ex-plains that "all that lives is endowed with the essence of the Bud-dha" and, like other world traditions, it compares that essence to gold. Gold, it says, is indestructible in nature. If it were cast into a place filled with impurities, it would remain the same, even after hundreds of years. The real part of us is like that gold. While it might become covered over by the muck and mire of life, it remains precious, pure, and indestructible. The influential Christian thinker Origen of Alexandria sounded a similar theme when he said that the divine "seed" within us can be "covered over and hidden, but never destroyed or extinguished in itself; it glows and gleams, shines and burns and inclines without ceasing towards God."

While the sages continually draw our attention back to this golden essence of ours, they are also realists. They don't deny that when we are walking off the beaten path or fighting in the trenches of life, we will get dirty. When we are standing under a storm cloud, we will get drenched. Accept that, they tell us; it's part of life. Just don't forget that underneath it all you are made of solid gold.

Unfortunately, over centuries and millennia, that universal truth has itself become hidden from view. Some of the fanatical followers of the great teachers departed from the original teachings they had received. Those followers decided to focus so much on the mud that sticks to the surface that after a while they, and we, forgot that there was a divine spark, a golden fire, abiding within us. The glow of that fire is what is meant to shine through us as we move about our daily lives. That is what we honor in ourselves.

Honoring yourself, then, is honoring your Self, with a capital S. When you honor your Self, you are dedicated to expressing your best nature. When you honor your Self, you stoke the fire within. The brighter that blaze, the more it can warm others and light the way for them so that they, too, can discover their own inner light.

Since criticism comes so easily, from both within and without, it's essential to find ways to remind yourself to focus on the presence of the sun within rather than the clouds passing overhead that temporarily eclipse its brilliance. I stumbled on a small but effective strategy when I was in a brooding mood one evening. I had been blaming myself for problems I was having at work. Not only were these particular situations hopeless, I told myself, but so was I. This mess was all my fault. What was wrong with me that I attracted these painful situations?

I went for a walk alone as twilight was nearing. Nature began to work its magic on me, as it always does, and I couldn't help but say to myself, *"How beautiful is everything God makes!"* And then I heard in my heart, like an echo coming back to me, *"So you must be beautiful too."* It was as if a light had suddenly illumined the darkness, and, despite my foul mood, I caught a glimpse of the gold inside of me. That little dose of truth gave me the strength to keep going. It reminded me that there was not something inherently wrong with me, even if I stumbled here and there. It also helped me see that judging myself wasn't doing me or anyone else a bit of good. It restored my hope that things could get better—and that I was better than I was giving myself credit for.

THE GREAT ESCAPE

Even though we may know that we have magnificence inside of us and that it is essential to play the leading role in our lives, we may still find ourselves anywhere else but center stage. You could call it the great escape—keeping ourselves so busy taking care of everyone else that we don't take the time to help ourselves or express our own greatness. It sounds ridiculous to want to escape from that. Who would want to run away from the opportunity to be great?

Lots of us, according to the prominent twentieth-century psychologist Abraham Maslow. He calls our urge to run from our greatness "the Jonah complex," after the prophet Jonah, that great escape artist who tried to elude his destiny. The story of Jonah goes like this. God commands Jonah, an Israelite, to

warn the people of the city of Nineveh to repent of their wicked-
ness. Jonah is not happy about this assignment. The Ninevites
are the enemies of his people. Why should he help save them?
He tries to run from his assignment by boarding a ship headed
in the opposite direction, but a violent storm erupts and the
sailors are forced to throw him overboard to calm the sea. A
great fish swallows Jonah, and after three days spits him onto
dry land, but only after the prophet repents and asks for mercy.
At last, Jonah gets the message: you can run but you cannot hide
from your calling. This time, when God asks him to preach to
the people in Nineveh, he obeys, warning them that the city will
be destroyed in forty days. All the people of that city, including
the king himself, take Jonah's message to heart. They choose to
fast, call on God, and turn from their violent ways. As a result,
what Jonah feared comes to pass—the city is spared.

Underlying Jonah's adventures, so like our own, are several
intriguing paradoxes, which, as you can guess, is the whole
point of the story. For one, God is asking Jonah to save the very
people who are his so-called enemies. Secondly, God doesn't fit
into Jonah's neat little box of what a "God" should behave like.
Then, as now, some people envisioned God as a giant judge with
a sledgehammer whose job was to angrily stamp out their enemies. Yet in this episode, God is more tender and compassionate than the judgmental prophet, who wants to decide for himself
who should and should not be saved. Last but not least, Jonah
plays the part of both a great prophet called to fulfill a mighty
mission and a rebellious runaway who needs a reality check.

It turns out that many of us are like Jonah, especially when
it comes to that last part about being the rebellious runaway.
We have the same urges to run from our task in life, to escape
our true vocation. We sense our great potential, but we also
doubt that we can live up to those grand expectations. We start

adding up our character flaws and run out of fingers and toes to count them on. We get anxious that we won't be able to deliver.

The Jonah complex is not hard to detect. It revealed itself every time Maslow asked his students who among them was hoping to write the great American novel or become an outstanding composer, a senator, or even the president. His students would giggle, blush, and squirm (what would you do?), and Maslow responded by saying, "If not you, then who else?"

He pushed his graduate students toward higher levels of aspiration by delivering this little speech to them, one that echoes, in part, the theme of this book: "Are you in training to be a mute or an inactive psychologist? What's the advantage of that? That's not a good path to self-actualization. No, you must want to be a first-class psychologist, meaning the best, the very best you are capable of becoming. If you deliberately plan to be less than you are capable of being, then I warn you that you'll be deeply unhappy for the rest of your life."[4] Author Marianne Williamson describes the same syndrome of self-doubt in her book *A Return to Love*, where she writes, "We ask ourselves, Who am I to be brilliant, gorgeous, talented, fabulous? Actually, who are you *not* to be? You are a child of God. Your playing small doesn't serve the world."[5]

If you let the fear that you won't be able to live up to your great potential get the upper hand, you may find yourself doing any or all of the following. You may convince yourself that any bright ideas you have for sharing your gifts are just delusional dreams. You may say, "Who? Me?" and promptly run in the other direction. You may devalue yourself in front of others or set low expectations for yourself. You may pretend to be weak or inept so you won't have to face your fears, take risks, or deal with disappointments. You may become an escape artist, melting into a life of mediocrity where you won't have to step out onto center stage and take the starring role in your life.

Your stage fright may cause you to do what I mentioned at the start of this section—fill your time with so many obligations to fulfill for others that you don't have the energy or drive left over to mine your own gold. You might volunteer to fight other people's battles or support their causes as a way to avoid the angst of grappling with your own assignments in life. But these strategies never work. No matter how noble a task may be, if it is not your own, it is merely a distraction. Being less than your brightest self only brings emptiness and unhappiness.

MYTH:
Who? Me? I can't be great if I have shortcomings.

MAGIC:
*I may have weaknesses, but I am also wonderful.
Doubts will come and go, but I won't let them
keep me from giving my gifts.*

Are you gun-shy of your own greatness? Do you demean yourself so you won't have to do what it takes to give your gifts? Do you try to escape from your potential for greatness by convincing yourself that you can't even hope to begin a project because you won't be able to do it "perfectly"? Once again, the Bhagavad Gita sets the record straight. In that dramatic battlefield dialogue, Krishna tells Arjuna: "Action is greater than inaction: perform therefore thy task in life. . . . A man should not abandon his work, even if he cannot achieve it in full perfection; because in all work there may be imperfection, even as in all fire there is smoke."[6]

All this points to one of life's most sublime paradoxes— we are both weak and wonderful. We have human limitations and superhuman potentials. We are both human *and* divine, and that requires us to have deep humility as well as deep self-respect and inner pride in our gifts.

One of the wisest and most courageous choices you will ever make is to acknowledge your current limitations and, at the same time, applaud your greatness. The fact that we have weaknesses is a given, and therefore it's natural at times to have doubts and feel unworthy. It's even healthy to acknowledge those feelings. The doubts will come and go, but don't let them paralyze you. Instead, embrace the paradox and dance.

SOME WILL UNDERSTAND

In this and the last two chapters, I have talked about several of the myths and obstacles that can keep you from celebrating your own voice and giving your gifts. There is one more that deserves our attention here. It's an obstacle that can hover below the surface of our conscious awareness without us ever realizing that it is there. We may make the choice not to honor ourselves or give our gifts because we fear that we'll be misunderstood, rejected, or maligned.

In reality, everyone who has resisted the current of conformity and challenged the status quo in any arena, personal or professional, has at one time or another been misunderstood. As Emerson points out, "Pythagoras was misunderstood, and Socrates, and Jesus, and Luther, and Copernicus, and Galileo, and Newton, and every pure and wise spirit that ever took flesh. To be great is to be misunderstood."

Whenever we attempt to break out of the conventional to express our authentic voice, we can expect to draw some fire. It comes with the territory. That fire serves an important purpose.

It compels us to summon our own inner fire as we stand for what we know is right. The world's traditions are filled with stories that demonstrate how resistance from outside can create just the right conditions for an inner breakthrough. As the following archetypal example from Eastern tradition shows, challenges can be the very thing we need to catapult us to a new level. (You may be familiar with this scene, as it was portrayed in the movie *Little Buddha*, featuring Keanu Reeves.)

In chapter 2, I told the story of Siddhartha Gautama, the Indian prince who left his throne and family in search of enlightenment. For years, he practiced harsh austerities, thinking that this would bring him closer to his goal, but he became so weak that he fainted and almost died. When a young girl fed him a bowl of rich rice milk, he regained his strength. Fortified by his simple meal, Gautama was determined to sit beneath a tree and meditate until he achieved enlightenment.

Once Gautama sat down under that tree, he was faced with challenge after challenge. Mara, the Tempter, summoned all kinds of temptations to lure Gautama away from that spot and distract him from his reason for being, much as Jesus was tempted in the wilderness and many saints were mocked and harangued as they prayed, meditated, or tried to sleep. Mara sent his seductive daughters to tempt Gautama. Mara besieged him with horrific demons, storms, and vicious attacks. Worse than all of this, Mara challenged Gautama's right to be doing what he was doing and to be who he was. In fact, Mara had the audacity to claim that it was he, not Gautama, who should be seated on the throne of enlightenment. Tradition says that throughout it all, Gautama remained unmoved. Finally, he took his right hand, reached down, and with the tips of his fingers touched the ground in front of him, summoning the earth to witness to and affirm his right to pursue his path. In response, the earth thunderously roared, "I bear you witness." Mara and his armies fled.

After spending the night alone in deep meditation, Gautama at last attained his goal of enlightenment. He had become the Buddha, meaning the "enlightened one" or, more literally, the "awakened one"—the one who has awakened to the true nature of reality and to the reality of his true inner nature. He had come to experience firsthand the truth that we all have that indestructible golden essence inside of us. But Mara was not finished with him yet. He had one last trick in his bag. He told Gautama, "Don't bother returning to the world. No one will understand your teaching or your experience. Why not leave the world behind and slip into nirvana forever?"

That must have been a difficult test. Who would not want to be forever free of the human condition, its pettiness, and its unpredictable challenges? "Is Mara right? Will I be able to translate my profound experiences into words? And will anyone really understand what I have to say?"—all these thoughts and more certainly went through Gautama's head. But he also thought about all the people, then and in the future, who would continue suffering in ignorance if he did not get up from under that tree and teach them what he had learned about suffering and how to put an end to it. He knew that he must share his insights, even if he could help only one or two people. So Gautama answered Mara with the words we must all speak into the face of the taunters and tempters who try to unseat us: *"Some will understand."* When he spoke those words, Mara disappeared.

We tend to look at the great figures of history, or even people today who excel in their fields, and think that they never faced the challenges we do. That's not true. They faced the same doubts and fears, but they moved forward and gave their gifts in spite of them. They heard the doubting and condemning voices but decided to obey their own true voice. They chose to honor themselves.

You, too, may have heard the taunting refrains of the tempter as you contemplated what steps you could take to share your gifts, whether at home, at work, or in your community. As a result, you may have said to yourself: "Why bother putting myself on the line? There are so many obstacles. It's too hard. It's not worth it. My family and friends don't understand. Nobody will appreciate my efforts. Besides, I'm not sure anybody will be interested in what I have to say." If you hear those thoughts emerging again, now you will know who they are coming from and how to reply: *Some will understand, and so I will give my gifts.*

------ 🕊 ------

MYTH:
Why bother? No one will understand
what I am trying to say or do.

MAGIC:
Someone will understand what I have to
say and value what I have to share,
and so I will give my gifts.

If you want to make the most of your life, you will have to confront the same questions that everyone who boldly chooses to give their gifts must face: Will I allow anyone or anything to pull me away from my goal? Will I let myself be convinced that I am not talented enough, organized enough, perfect enough, strong enough, beautiful enough, rich enough, or articulate enough to do what my heart is telling me to do? Or will I stand my ground and remind myself that I do not have to be perfect to pursue my calling? When confronted with the audacity of the cynics and the critics, will I look into my heart and summon the audacity to go ahead and give anyway?

A saying from the Hasidic tradition sums up the challenge and the antidote: "Shall men, then, always walk in meekness? Not so, say the Masters. There are moments when haughtiness becomes a duty. When the Evil Inclination approaches, whispering in the ear: 'You are unworthy to fulfill the Law,' say: 'I am worthy.' "

KEYS TO THE
BALANCING ACT

Seven Strategies to
Keep Voting for Yourself

"Journey within yourself," wrote the Sufi poet Rumi. "Enter a mine of rubies and bathe in the splendor of your own light."[7] Each of us has magnificence inside of us. The challenge is to keep on celebrating that shining part of you even when the storm clouds of life move in and momentarily eclipse its brilliance. The following seven strategies can help you to honor your inner radiance and to keep voting for yourself no matter what is happening around you.

❶ Write a love letter to yourself. Pretend for a moment that you are your own greatest advocate. Now write a supportive and encouraging note to yourself as if you were cheering yourself on. Then pop it in an envelope and mail it to yourself. When you are traveling, send a postcard with an inspiring message to your home address. Right before shutting down your e-mail for the night, send yourself a note of appreciation so that you will see it when you download your e-mail the next day. Develop the habit of applauding your greatness.

❷ Personalize your screen saver. Put the screen saver on your computer monitor to good use. Set it to show images or affirmations that counteract the negative or doubting voices within and without. Be specific and address what you are currently focusing on in your life. For example, you can set your screen saver to display reminders like "I take great care of myself because I deserve to be happy and healthy," "I have something important to say and I say it with confidence and ease," or simply "I honor myself every day by_____" and then fill in the blank with what is most important for you right now.

❸ Keep a photo of yourself as a child nearby. Choose a photo of yourself as a child that reminds you of your innate joy, sweetness, curiosity, or love of life—a photo that reflects who you really are at heart. Buy a beautiful frame for it and place the photo somewhere where you can view it often. Every time you see it, let that heart-opening image put you back in touch with the precious part of yourself that reflects back to you your real essence.

❹ Hang out with people who celebrate and support who you are. Period. If you allow yourself to be pressured or pummeled by someone who doesn't appreciate your gifts, you will only be in a constant battle that will eat away at your energy and enthusiasm. You don't have to prove yourself to anyone or justify your dreams and plans. Your job is to be you.

❺ Use your windshield wiper. You would never risk driving a car in bad weather without windshield wipers. In everyday life, you also need a windshield wiper to clear away the frustrations, criticisms, and self-doubts that, like heavy rain or mud, can obscure your vision and make it hard to get where you are going. You may not be able to stop the rain that falls into your life, but you can turn on your windshield wiper. When you're feeling upset or when others aren't honoring the gold within you, what helps you see clearly again? Is it taking some time alone? Meditation or prayer? Journaling? Exercise? Walking in nature? Watching an inspiring movie? Talking to a supportive friend? Scheduling a massage or a session with a life coach? Make a list of the tools that work for you so you don't forget to put them into action when the storm clouds let loose.

6 **Act on your greatness.** Every one of us is weak in some way and wonderful in some way. If you acted on your greatness, how would you give your gifts to others? What would you do to increase your capacity to give? Write down the answers to those questions and then ask yourself each week: *What one step can I take, even if it's a small one, to celebrate my greatness, develop my gifts, and give more of myself to others?*

7 **Create an arsenal of affirmations.** The best defense is a good offense. Doubts and detractors may try to unseat you, but you can be prepared ahead of time with the truth. Write down two or more affirmations to say aloud or to yourself to counter the doubts or criticisms that may well up inside of you or come from others. Create affirmations that apply specifically to the issues you are dealing with in your life. Here are some examples: "I am a magnificent being in the process of becoming ever more magnificent." "My job is not to be perfect but to be the best I can be right now." "Someone will understand what I have to say and value what I have to share, and so I will give my gifts." When the barrage comes, turn to your list and fire away with conviction in your heart.

CHAPTER 15

BROADENING YOUR VISION *of the* POSSIBLE

Seeing. We might say that the
whole of life lies in that verb.
—PIERRE TEILHARD DE CHARDIN

One afternoon, Nasrudin, the Sufi sage we met earlier, discovered an odd-looking bird on his window sill. It was, in fact, the king's hawk. Since Nasrudin has never seen such a bird before, he thinks it is simply a mis-shapen pigeon. Before long, Nasrudin is busy clipping the bird's talons. Next, he cuts its regal beak to make it look straighter. Finishing his job, he releases the bird, exclaiming, "Someone's been neglecting you. Now you look more like a bird!"

Haven't we all done the same when a new idea, per-spective, or personality has tried to squeeze itself into our existing pigeon holes of thinking, and we've expelled what didn't fit before it could change us? How many times in a lifetime or even a day are we called to change the shape of our mental molds so we can fit something new inside, whether it comes from our children, parents, siblings, spouses, co-workers, neighbors, or various groups and political parties who think, act, or see the world differently than we do?

Learning to appreciate another's point of view is essential, and not just because we must all share the same patch of planet in this solar system. It's also important because of this profound personal truth: *when I adjust my perspective to include a wider range of what is possible in the world around me, I automatically broaden my vision of what is possible for me.* If we think that everyone must look like a pigeon, we'll never be able to imagine ourselves as a majestic hawk.

Carol discovered this truth after years of struggling to accept that her daughter, Lynn, had chosen a different faith than her own. Although Carol and her husband had raised their daughter in the orthodox Jewish tradition, when Lynn was in her late teens she began looking into other traditions that inspired her. She was grateful for her Jewish roots but felt drawn to a different spiritual practice. Over the years, she and her parents simply stopped talking about it. After her father had passed on, Lynn was visiting her mother one day and, in a rare moment of candor, Carol expressed the feelings she had kept bottled up all those years. "I'm sorry you rejected your father and me and our lifestyle," Carol blurted out. Lynn's eyes opened wide in surprise, and then in a soft, compassionate voice she said, "Mom, I didn't reject you and Daddy. I just had to be me."

Now it was Carol's turn to be surprised. For decades, she and her husband had believed that their daughter's different spiritual outlook was not only a rejection of them but a putdown. They felt they had done something terribly wrong in raising their daughter. Lynn's response helped Carol to see that she and her husband hadn't failed as parents and that her daughter was neither rebellious nor critical. She began to understand that Lynn hadn't been judging them at all; she was simply following her own heart.

Underneath her old feelings of resentment, Carol had been living with the myth that "if my daughter's choice is right, then my choice must be wrong." Like Carol, we sometimes think that other people's choices have to be wrong in order for our choices to be right for us. But by now you know that's not true. Life is thoroughly paradoxical. It calls us to let go of "either/or" and embrace "both."

❧

MYTH:
If I'm right, others must be wrong.

MAGIC:
Others' choices can be right for them and my choices can be right for me. When I honor new perspectives, I also broaden my vision of what is possible for me.

Depends on the circumstances

When Carol could finally embrace the paradox—when she was able to honor her daughter's choice as well as her own—something changed inside of her. Carol began to spread her wings. She enrolled in some classes and found new friends. She was happier. She even started seeing a psychologist to better understand herself and her feelings.

Respecting another's point of view does not mean you must agree with that person's choice or make that choice yourself. You can honor someone else's choices and, at the same time, honor your own path. There is room enough in the world and in your heart for both.

BY HONORING OTHERS, YOU HONOR YOURSELF

A wonderful legend related by the Russian novelist Leo Tolstoy in 1886 reinforces the lesson that we can never assume that our chosen lifestyle or way of doing things is better than another's, and that if we do, we only narrow our vision of what is possible for us. One day a bishop hears of three hermits who live alone on an island and decides to visit them. The boatman tries to discourage the bishop from doing this, saying, "I have heard say that they are foolish old fellows who understand nothing and never speak a word." The bishop insists on being taken to them. Since the ship cannot get too close to the island, he must be rowed ashore in a smaller boat. When he arrives, he introduces himself to the three old hermits and tells them that he wishes to teach them.

"Tell me," says the bishop, "what are you doing to save your souls, and how do you serve God on this island?"

One of the three answers, "We do not know how to serve God. We only serve and support ourselves, servant of God."

"But how do you pray?" asks the bishop.

"We pray in this way," replies the hermit. "Three are ye, three are we, have mercy upon us."

The bishop smiles and responds, "I see you wish to please the Lord, but you do not know how to serve Him." He then begins to teach them the "right way" to pray as instructed in the scriptures. Starting with "Our Father," the bishop has the hermits repeat the lines of the prayer after him, over and over again. All day, he patiently corrects them each time they blunder until all three can say the prayer by heart.

By the time the bishop is ready to leave, it is dark and the moon is rising. As the hermits bow down before the bishop, thanking him, he reminds them one last time to pray as he has taught them and then boards his boat. Slowly, the boat pulls away from the shore, making its way to the waiting ship. Once aboard the vessel, the sails are unfurled and the ship moves farther and farther out to sea until the bishop can no longer see the hermits or their little island.

Suddenly the bishop notices something white and shining moving quickly toward the boat. He tries to figure out exactly what he is seeing—a bird, a boat, a fish?—when into view come the three hermits, gliding across the water without moving their feet. When the three old men reach the boat, as if in unison they say to their shocked mentor: "We have forgotten your teaching, servant of God. As long as we kept repeating it, we remembered, but when we stopped saying it for a time, a word dropped out, and now it has all gone to pieces. We can remember nothing of it. Teach us again."

Crossing himself, the humbled bishop leans over the side of the ship and says, "Your own prayer will reach the Lord, men of God. It is not for me to teach you. Pray for us sinners." This time, it is the bishop who bows low before the old men, who turn around and glide across the sea to their home.

When we don't encourage others to make their own choices and follow their own stars, it's not just they who suffer. We all suffer when, as a couple, a family, an organization, a work group, a community, or a nation, we expect and breed conformity. We all suffer when we dishonor the gifts that others have been born to give—because we need those gifts. A moving apology offered in 1986 by the United Church of Canada to the Native Canadians expresses that sentiment and reminds me of the message of Tolstoy's fable. In part, that courageous and inspiring statement read: "Long before my people journeyed to this land your people were here and you received from your Elders an understanding of creation, and of the Mystery that surrounds us all that was deep, and rich, and to be treasured. We did not hear you when you shared your vision. . . . We tried to make you be like us and in so doing we helped to destroy the vision that made you what you were. As a result, you, and we, are poorer, and the image of the Creator in us is twisted, blurred, and we are not what we are meant by God to be. We ask you to forgive us."

Of course, when we are confronted by those who are critical of us, it can be difficult to let go of the need to make them wrong so that we can feel right. It's not always easy to remember the value of honoring others when they are not honoring us. We can get so involved in defending our right to be who we are that we become like the thing we are fighting against—intolerant and judgmental. Tomas found himself getting caught in that pattern, fed by years of tension between himself and his brother, Felipe. Both are extremely creative and talented, but you would never guess that they are brothers.

From outer appearances, the two couldn't look or act more differently. Felipe is an accomplished and well-paid Broadway choreographer while Tomas leads a simpler, quieter lifestyle in the open spaces of the West, where he works as a carpenter and pursues his talents as an artist on the side. At family gatherings, Felipe would subtly, and sometimes not so subtly, judge Tomas for his lack of money and worldly success. Tomas, normally a sweet, gentle man, would become highly defensive when he felt the sting of his brother's criticism. He, in turn, thought his brother was superficial and arrogant.

This saga had been going on for some time when Tomas shared it with me. "My brother has never approved of my lifestyle," he complained. It was obvious that there were unspoken rivalries between the two. I also suspected that both brothers were actually a bit insecure about their chosen paths, and in order to feel better about their choices they belittled each other. As Tomas continued telling me his story, at one point I wondered aloud, "Did you ever tell your brother that you are okay with the lifestyle he has chosen and that you are happy that he has found the success he's looking for? Or do you make him feel that you are better than he is?" After all, wasn't Tomas treating his brother the same way he detested being treated?

Tomas was silent for a moment. "I guess I'm so busy defending myself that I never really made Felipe feel that he had something to be proud of," he admitted. Tomas was beginning to see that while he felt judged and boxed in by the label his brother had given him ("professionally unaccomplished and financially unsuccessful"), he had been labeling his brother with judgments that were equally hurtful ("smug and not very spiritual"). They were at opposite ends of a tug of war and neither one would let go of the rope.

When I saw Tomas again some months later, he excitedly told me that he had recently returned from visiting his parents and had seen his brother. Tomas had made a conscious decision that he would honor his brother's choices just as he wished to be honored for his own. Instead of bracing himself to react to his brother's jibes, Tomas went out of his way to ask Felipe about his career and congratulate him on new accomplishments. There was still some tension between them, but the two got along better than they had in years. In talking to Tomas, I sensed that he was also more at peace about his own choices. The internal tug of war wasn't as intense. By giving his brother permission to be himself, Tomas was more comfortable being himself too.

LETTING YOUR CREATIVE SPIRIT SPEAK

Broadening our vision of what is possible often entails letting go of expectations—letting go of what we think others should be like and letting go of expectations we hold for ourselves. The celebrated American author Madeleine L'Engle, who wrote *A Wrinkle in Time*, reflected in her journal that "a self is not something static, tied up in a pretty parcel and handed to the child, finished and complete. A self is always becoming."[1] The freedom to *become*—what a precious gift to give our children rather than demanding that, like clones, they match our mental models of who they should be. What a precious gift to give ourselves as we honor our own process of becoming.

Guidelines are necessary and helpful in life, and we all need them, but ironclad expectations that go above and beyond the call of duty only close us down. As children and adults, we all need space, free from the clutter of other voices, to hear what our own true voice is leading us to do. When the demanding voices of expectation become too loud, we are no longer able to hear that voice, let alone follow it.

In his work, Abraham Maslow found that connecting with our inner voice is extremely important. He noted that people who are psychologically strong and healthy are "able to hear their inner-feeling-voices more clearly than most people." They use internal not external criteria when making their decisions, everything from what to eat or wear to issues of values and ethics. They are clear on what they do and do not want. Unfortunately, he says, the way we are raised often produces the opposite effect.

"Most of us," says Maslow, "have learned to avoid authenticity" and are therefore confused about that voice inside of us. We're trained to ignore our inner signals; we suppress our feelings rather than express them. He uses the example of the child who says he detests spinach but whose feelings are nullified by his mother, who tells him, "We love spinach," when she could just as easily have said, "I know you don't like spinach, but you have to eat it anyway for such-and-such reasons."[2]

If we don't encourage our children and ourselves to get in touch with our inner knowing and our deepest desires, we will eventually lose contact with the vital inner spirit that is the well-spring of truth within us. When that supremely sensitive and wise part of us can no longer breathe, it will fight back. If you blindly obey the voices outside of you, don't be surprised when your real self creates a commotion in your body, mind, or emotions to draw your attention back to what's happening inside of you.

Do not rush by this point. It is key. We tend to attribute stress and anxiety to some ineluctable, fast-paced force of modern life. But anxiety, depression, stress, and rebellion can be the outer manifestation of the tension that churns within us when we have taken on an identity that is not our own.

A friend told me about one of her son's schoolmates, Aaron, who exemplified this dynamic. The young teenager was smart, polite, and always perfectly behaved. Not only was he the model of a "perfect" child, but he also excelled at everything. He had already garnered a long list of awards and extracurricular achievements. His parents and teachers knew he was destined for great things. But my friend's son predicted that Aaron was actually headed for disaster because he wasn't being "real." Everything, from his smile to the way he dressed to the way he spoke to adults was artificial, as if he was acting out someone else's life and not his own.

A year later, Aaron made a sharp 180-degree turn. He went from getting straight As to failing all his classes, from total obedience to total rebellion. His parents were in shock. Without realizing it, their very precise expectations had left their son no room to breathe—no room to figure out what he liked and what he wanted. They had created a time bomb; their son had to explode, and with enough force, to break out of the mold and discover himself.

In a less drastic but no less significant way, Lauren, a single mother with two teenagers, broke out of the confines of her narrow expectations when she began to let her own creative spirit speak. I met Lauren when she came to my husband and me as publishing coaches to help her figure out how to turn her dream of publishing a book into a reality. She was passionate about her topic and said that she eventually wanted to devote herself entirely to giving talks and seminars on it. Lauren said she didn't have much time to devote to her project because she was a single mom and she worked full time. She was an enthusiastic person, but a part of her was also weary and frustrated. She told us that the one big obstacle in her life was that she hated her current job as well as the long commute that went with it. Both were exhausting her.

The more we worked with Lauren to explore how she could realistically move toward her goals with her available resources, the more she got in touch with her passion for the project. At the same time, those parts of her life that were not aligned with that passion were becoming more and more uncomfortable for her. The commotion inside of her was getting louder. Not long after we started working together, she unexpectedly announced to us that she had given her two-week notice at work and was quitting her job. She couldn't handle it any longer, she said, and would be looking for a new job.

This was, in fact, a good sign. Lauren was taking a daring step to create much-needed change. She was challenging an old belief that said, "I have to work at this job, even though it makes me very unhappy, because I have no other choice." You may be thinking, as I first did, that Lauren would now stop working on her book. Instead, she discarded another assumption that was holding her back—the idea that "I must either work at my job or pursue my real passion." She embraced the paradox and did both. In between job hunting and a part-time job, Lauren continued to work on her project. Her long-range goal was to get the framework of a good book proposal in place to send out to publishers. In the meantime, she started by creating an e-book from her material. Her energy was incredible. Connecting to her inner voice and freeing herself from outworn assumptions had unleashed a lot of pent-up energy that she could now channel into fulfilling her dreams.

Lauren was not impractical. She knew that she couldn't afford to devote herself full time to her project at the moment, but she refused to get stuck in black-and-white, either/or thinking. Rather than shut down in the face of her job challenge and starve her passion, she nurtured it a little bit every week. And, like everything we nurture, that passion grew healthier and stronger. You have the same choice. You can conform to what you think is doable or you can break out of that mindset, listen to your inner spirit, and redefine what is possible for you.

MAKING THE CONNECTION AND TRUSTING YOURSELF

We all have different ways of making and sustaining the connection with our inner spirit and hearing our true voice. For me, roaming in nature, where nothing but authenticity abounds, immediately reconnects me to my real self. Have you ever seen a lilac bush trying to be an apple tree, or an ant pretending to be a bee? Some people prefer to reconnect through some form of quiet reflection, meditation, or prayer, while others use yoga or dream work. It doesn't matter which tool you use to open a space so that you can hear your inner voice. What matters is that you use what works for you when you need it.

Someone I know uses her dreams to help her connect with her inner guidance. This story is not about the technique she used, since what works for one person doesn't work for everyone, but about how reconnecting to her own inner voice changed her life. For years, Michele had worked as an executive assistant, but she no longer enjoyed that kind of work. What excited her now was graphic design. She had taken some design classes, was very talented, and had even done some freelance work on the side. She felt a strong pull to move into that field, but with little real-world experience, she was unsure of herself. So rather than changing her expectations and moving closer to her real desires, she left her job as an executive assistant and accepted another job doing the same thing but for another company. The night before she was to begin her new job, Michele started feeling anxious. Before she went to bed, she asked for a dream to show her why. That night, she dreamed that she was walking around a campfire, saying over and over, "I don't want to lose my soul yet. I don't want to lose my soul yet."

When she remembered the dream the next morning, she thought that it seemed a little overdramatic. "Maybe that's not really a message from my soul," she told herself. Michele talked herself into believing that the dream was just a reflection of the normal jitters that everyone gets when starting a new job. Ten months later, however, she was right back where she had started. She was having trouble sleeping and dreaded getting out of bed each morning to go to work. She was bored and unhappy. When Michele started getting severe headaches, she knew that she had to listen to what her inner spirit had been trying to tell her all along. She made up her mind to quit her job in two weeks, whether or not she had a new one lined up. And she promised herself that she would never again apply for a job that she knew would leave her unfulfilled.

Within a few days of making that decision, an amazing thing happened. Michele received a phone call from her old design teacher, who asked her if she was free to help him with some freelance jobs that might turn into steady work. Now she could do the work she loved and get training on the job. It took one more encounter, though, for Michele to totally trust that she had made the right decision. A month into her freelance work, she received an offer for a full-time job managing the office at an art school, where she had applied to work the last time she was job hunting. Faced with this new choice, her old doubts crept in. Her logical mind was telling her that since there was no guarantee that the freelance work would continue, this new job offered more security. Michele felt confused. She asked for another dream to help her make up her mind.

This time, she dreamed about a goldfish whose head kept popping out of the water. In the dream, she had to keep pushing its head underwater to keep it safe and alive. "To me, the message was clear," Michele said as she shared this story with me. "I would be a fish out of water if I took this new job." That kind of work simply wasn't a good fit for her any longer.

———— 🌿 ————

MYTH:
*Logic and practical evaluation
will lead me to the truth.*

MAGIC:
*Logic has its place, but to make the best decisions
I must also listen to my inner voice and trust myself.*

The dream affirmed what she already knew in her heart—that if she didn't follow her inner promptings, she would be spending another ten months and then another ten years unfulfilled and unhappy. Logic certainly has its place, but it is only one side of the paradox. To make the best decisions, we also have to honor our creative spirit and trust its guidance.

Underneath Michele's doubts was another pattern, one that I can relate to and perhaps you can too. Right next to the voice of the real self is a voice that tries to convince us that if we misstep or if we don't jump at an opportunity that has landed on our doorsteps, we will never get another chance. If we don't jump now, it tells us, we'll be sorry for the rest of our lives. That's rarely the case. Those fearful voices that shout "last chance, last chance" are as silly as those ads that say "last chance to save," as if we will never ever find another sale on curtains, cookery, or designer clothing. Michele now knows that listening to the fearful voice has caused her to take steps that aren't headed in the right direction for her. "But my real feelings, my intuition," she says, "have *never* let me down."

The more you practice listening for your real voice, the better you will become at telling the difference between it and the voice of your fears. In my own ongoing process of learning to pay attention to my true inner voice, I've found that it helps immensely to literally *listen to my voice*—to listen to how I am speaking rather than what I am saying. We use this skill all the time to read others. We know that a friend is upset or burdened when we hear her voice crack. We know that our children are happy when they are animated and speak quickly. If we call a parent and we hear a listless, dull voice at the other end of the phone, we know something is wrong. It's not the words that tell us but the expression in the voice. The tone tells it all.

While we're accustomed to reading others in this way, we can get so caught up in what's happening around us that we forget to listen to ourselves. Yet that is exactly what gives us valuable clues for getting back on track. If, for instance, you catch yourself sounding grumpy, impatient, or tired, it's probably time to ask, "What am I feeling, and what can I do to honor myself right now?" If you hear a worried or frantic tone in your voice, that may be a sign that you need to slow down and get back in touch with the present moment rather than letting speculative fears of the future spin you out of control. Your voice holds valuable messages if you listen for them—and it's not just the downturns that speak to us. When you catch that lilt of excitement in your voice or when you hear yourself happily whistling or humming away, take note. What are you doing or thinking about that is making your heart sing? That's what can bring more joy into your life when you do it again and again.

COMMITTING TO WHAT'S IMPORTANT

What does your creative spirit tell you and are you in touch with what makes you excited to be alive? Are you being honest about what your inner voice is saying, and are you committed to following through on it? Almost overnight, being honest changed the life of a woman I met several years ago. For years, Jan had lived in Florida to be near her family. She used to love living there, but things had changed quite a bit since she first arrived. It was one of the most rapidly growing and annoyingly busy areas of the state. Fighting her way through heavy traffic every day was a ritual she had come to detest. Jan felt an obligation to stay near her aging parents, but living and working in an environment she did not enjoy was taking its toll.

One day in a moment of supreme frustration, Jan's inner voice, which had been drowned out by the noise and sheer busyness of her life, broke through to her conscious awareness. She was stuck in traffic once again, bitterly reciting her usual litany of complaints, when she heard herself say aloud: "If I only had six months to live, where would I go and what would I do?"

Instantly, she knew the answer. Her favorite place on earth was Montana, where she had been vacationing with her parents every summer for years. "That's where I would be if I had six months to live!" she said to herself. "What am I waiting for?" In that flash of insight, Jan suddenly saw that she had been living with the lie that "I can wait until tomorrow to be happy," which is another way of saying, "I can wait to be me."

Listening to your true inner voice does not, of course, mean you should abandon your duty to others and act irresponsibly. The paradox of giving and receiving call us to balance both factors. Jan knew this. She was keenly aware of her obligation to her parents. She didn't fly off without first checking to make sure her parents would be okay without her. (And when her parents needed her help five years later, Jan honored the pendulum swing that was sweeping her to the other side of the paradox and readily returned to Florida to care for them.)

MYTH:
I can wait until tomorrow to be me.

MAGIC:
I can balance my obligations with what my inner spirit is guiding me to do. There's no better time to create the life I want than now.

When Jan first told her parents that she wanted to move to Montana, they could see that Jan desperately needed this change. They told her that they were more than happy to let her move into their tiny vacation home until she found a place of her own. It didn't take long to set the wheels of change in motion. Although Jan thought she would have a hard time finding jobs in her profession in the small town she was moving to, she quickly found a position not far away. She was surprised at how easily everything seemed to be falling into place. As she was wrapping up her plans, Jan got another surprise. She met and fell head over heels in love with Randy.

Was this just a cruel twist of fate? I don't think so. I've seen over and over again, in my own life and in the lives of others, that when we are in alignment with our true self, we automatically attract more of what we need and deserve. I believe that Jan and Randy found each other precisely because she had chosen to listen to and obey her inner voice.

Faced with what could quickly become a serious relationship, Jan was still committed to staying true to herself and to settling in a place where she could be happy. Realizing that she might never see Randy again, she reluctantly told him that she was moving ahead with her plans to leave Florida. Without a second thought, he responded, "I'm coming with you." Not long after the two moved to Montana and were married, another dream of Jan's came true—she became pregnant.

The transformation in Jan's life started with her single bold question—"If I only had six months to live, where would I go and what would I do?"—and her equally bold answer. Whenever you are willing to ask the question that is right for you and then listen closely to the answer that spontaneously arises in your heart, you are honoring your own voice. You are celebrating who you really are. And that never fails to create a beautiful chain reaction.

PLAYING WITH PARADOX AND GIVING YOUR GIFTS

Like the gatekeeper who demands that we speak the magic word before the sealed door will fly open and we can pass through, life is always asking us to solve the next riddle to create our next breakthrough. That riddle often comes in the form of a paradox, those two seemingly contradictory truths that challenge us to change our ways of being and seeing. Paradox, as you now know, is bent on teaching us that life is rarely filled with clear-cut choices between "this" or "that." Paradox asks us to embrace "this" *and* "that" so we can expand our capacity to give *and* to receive.

You don't have to look far for the paradox that will create your next breakthrough. It's right in front of you. It's smack in the middle of that sore spot in your life. If, for instance, you are allergic to saying no, even when saying yes is exhausting you, life will ask you to discover that the remedy lies in the opposite direction—in drawing good boundaries and embracing the paradox that saying no will enable you to keep saying yes. If you focus solely on your long-range goals, life will take you by the shoulders, spin you around, and make you look straight into the eyes of a loved one, where you cannot help but see that the present moment is as important as the big picture. If you cling to the notion that your happiness depends on what someone else says or does, life will eventually shake you free so that you can learn at last to trust yourself. And so it goes.

Knowing that life is a series of paradoxes dressed up in everyday clothes won't make life's tensions disappear; they are inevitable. But the sense of struggle we experience when we meet them is not. The excessive stress and strain come from staying stuck on one side or the other of the paradox. Leaning too much or too long to the right or the left only results in half-living. If it's full living you want, then it's paradox you must fully embrace. *Find the paradox at play, the sages urge, and play with paradox. Open your heart and you will broaden your vision of the possible.*

Whether we want to be enrolled or not, we are all students of the inner art of giving and receiving. In that classroom, the paradox at the heart of all others is "How do I honor myself *and* honor others? How do I balance what others need with what I need? How do I give *and* receive?" Ultimately, honoring yourself and honoring others, like the components of every good paradox, are inextricably woven together. Each one may take turns coming to the fore, but one cannot exist without the other, and therein lies the key. As we explored at the beginning of our journey into paradox, honoring yourself is not a self-centered pursuit. When you honor yourself, you are giving birth to your best self so that you can turn around and give creatively and abundantly to others. Conversely, and just as importantly, when you give to others, you also honor yourself. You honor what your heart was made to do. You honor your reason for being.

How can I give birth to my best self? What can I do to honor myself at the deepest levels so that I can creatively and abundantly give my gifts? Those are the questions that lie under and over and around all the other questions we may ask ourselves. One thing is for sure. To honor yourself fully, you must stop hiding behind sacrifice, fear, and doubt and start celebrating who you are. You must stop postponing the hot pursuit of your potential and start giving your gifts in a way that excites you.

When you give full reign to the passion that emanates from your creative spirit, the magic unfolds before your very eyes. You don't give because you are supposed to give, and you don't give just because someone else needs your gift. You give because that's what you were made to do. Because you can't do anything else. Because your cup is brimming over. I was inspired and motivated to write this book because I knew that what I was learning in my own life, sometimes painfully and sometimes joyfully, could help many others. But I also wrote this because I have to write—because I was born to do this.

What were you born to do? What qualities or talents are your special contribution to the world around you? And how

222

are you giving your gifts? Each of us will answer those questions differently. What will you say? The varieties are endless: I was born to teach. I was born to show others how important gratitude is in the face of tragedy. My gift is to help people look their best and build their confidence. I was born to nurture and heal. My gift is to show how compassion, in even the smallest of ways, can change the lives of others. I was born to organize and to lead. To bring joy and laughter wherever I go. To help others express themselves and share their unique gifts.

What is the quality of heart you are meant to share with others, not only because it will help them or because you will get something in return, but because you can't help it? It's who you are. It's what makes you smile and sets your heart on fire. When you are in touch with that deep, soulful urge that only you can fulfill, your priorities shift. You are no longer at the bottom of the pile, and the gifts you were born to share are no longer gasping for air. As the fire inside of you grows, you come to realize that there is only one way you can give your gift. And that is to honor yourself—every single day. Because, in reality, *you are the gift*.

ACKNOWLEDGMENTS

Whoever we are and whatever we create at any given moment is truly the celebration of all that has come before. So there is not enough room here to thank all the people in my life who have helped me become who I am. But I would be remiss if I did not express my profound gratitude to my beautiful parents, my precious grandparents, and my wonderful sisters for your loving hearts and for teaching me how to give with my heart.

I also offer my heartfelt thanks and gratitude to all those who stood by me and supported me through the process of giving birth to this book: To Theresa McNicholas, Lee Fogarty, Chris Kelley, Molly Maguire, Gabriel Wilmoth, Tina Knowles, Teresa Masterson, Marie Antoinette Kelley, and Tony Proe for giving me valuable feedback as the manuscript was taking shape and for cheering me on. To Roger Gefvert for the inspired cover design and James Bennett for the beautiful interior design, both of which capture the spirit and vision of this work. To Murray Steinman, Nilsa Abreu, and Brook Montagna for your support, friendship, and encouragement—and for helping me to honor endings so I could greet new beginnings. To friends and acquaintances I have met along life's way for sharing your stories that illumined the lessons in this book. To the sages of the world's inner traditions, past and present, for so generously opening your hearts and offering your wisdom, experience, and spiritual common sense to us all. Finally, to my husband, Nigel J. Yorwerth, not only for your expert advice and passionate work as my literary agent, but also for your enthusiastic belief in me, your deep friendship, and the inspiration of your love. And to Elizabeth Clare Prophet for teaching me, loving me, and showing me what courage is—and for broadening, ever broadening, my vision of the possible. Thank you all so much. I honor your hearts.

NOTES

Chapter 2 Seeking Balance
1. Nikos Kazantazakis, *Zorba the Greek*, trans. Carl Wildman (New York: Simon & Schuster, 1952), 34.
2. Mother Teresa, *In the Heart of the World: Thoughts, Stories & Prayers*, ed. Becky Benenate (Novato, CA: New World Library, 1997), 20-21.
3. Mother Teresa, *Everything Starts from Prayer: Mother Teresa's Meditations on Spiritual Life for People of All Faiths,* ed. Anthony Stern (Ashland, OR: White Cloud Press, 2000), 29.
4. The Book of Thomas the Contender in James M. Robinson, ed., *The Nag Hammadi Library in English,* rev. ed. (New York: HarperCollins, 1988), 201.
5. Daniel C. Matt, *The Essential Kabbalah: The Heart of Jewish Mysticism* (New York: HarperCollins, 1995), 127.

Chapter 3 Setting Boundaries
1. Rich Karlgaard, "Peter Drucker On Leadership," *Forbes.com,* Nov. 19, 2004, http://www.forbes.com/2004/11/19/cz_rk_1119drucker.html.
2. Rob Stein, "Study Confirms That Stress Helps Speed Aging," Washingonpost.com, posted on *MSNBC,* Nov. 30, 2004, http://www.msnbc.msn.com/id/6613721/.
3. Carol S. Pearson, *The Hero Within: Six Archetypes We Live By* (New York: HarperCollins, 1989), 53.
4. Ibid.
5. Alan Watts, *What Is Zen?*, in *Eastern Wisdom* (New York: MJF Books, 2000), 53.

Chapter 4   Accepting Support and Flying Solo
1. *New Era Community* (New York: Agni Yoga Society, 1951), 3.
2. Thich Nhat Hanh, *Living Buddha, Living Christ* (New York: Riverhead Books, 1995), 63-64.
3. Kahlil Gibran, *The Prophet* (Sydney: Phone Media), 15-16.

Chapter 5   Better than Bigger
1. Eric Fromm, *The Art of Loving* (New York: HarperCollins, 2000), 21-22.
2. The Bhagavad Gita 9:26 in Juan Mascaro trans., *The Bhagavad Gita* (New York: Penguin Books, 1962,), 82.

Chapter 6   What and When Do We Give?
1. Kahlil Gibran, *The Prophet* (Sydney: Phone Media), 20.
2. Malcolm Muggeridge, *Something Beautiful for God* (San Francisco: Harper & Row, 1971), 74-75.
3. Prabhavananda, *The Eternal Companion: Brahmananda, His Life and Teachings* (Hollywood: Vendanta Press, 1970), 73-74.
4. Thomas Cleary, trans. and ed., *Vitality, Energy, Spirit: A Taoist Sourcebook* (Boston: Shambhala Publications, 1991), 233.

Chapter 7   The Magic of Flow
1. Thomas A. Harris, *I'm OK—You're OK: A Practical Guide to Transactional Analysis* (New York: Harper & Row, 1969), 141.
2. David G. Myers, *Exploring Psychology: Sixth Edition in Modules* (New York: Worth Publishers, 2005), 442-43; David G. Myers, "Wealth, Well-Being, and the New American Dream, *Enough!* (Summer 2000), 5-6. See also David G. Myers, *The Pursuit of Happiness: Discovering the Pathway to Fulfillment, Well-Being, and Enduring Personal Joy* (New York: HarperCollins, 2002).
3. David G. Myers, "Pursuing Happiness," *Psychology Today,* July/August 1993, 32-35, 66-67.
4. Jean Chatsky, *You Don't Have to Be Rich: Comfort, Happiness, and Financial Security on Your Own Terms* (New York: Porfolio, 2003).
5. Arthur C. Brooks, "Giving Makes You Rich," *Condé Nast Portfolio,* November 2007.
6. Tao Te Ching 81.
7. 1 Timothy 6:10.
8. The Bhagavad Gita 3:11-12.

Chapter 8 Eyes Wide Open

1. See Jack Kornfield and Christina Feldman, eds., *Soul Food: Stories to Nourish the Spirit and the Heart* (San Francisco: HarperSanFrancisco, 1996), 274-75.
2. Adapted from Paul Carus, comp., *The Gospel of Buddha* (Oxford: Oneworld Publications, 1994), 167-68.

Chapter 9 Being Honest about Your Feelings

1. Rabindranath Tagore, *Stray Birds* (New York: The Macmillan Company, 1916).
2. Swami Vivekananda, *Jnana-Yoga*, rev. ed. (New York: Ramakrishna-Viveknanda Center, 1982), 286.
3. Jeffrey Brantley, *Calming Your Anxious Mind: How Mindfulness and Compassion Can Free You From Anxiety Fear, and Panic* (Oakland: New Harbinger Publications), 105, 153.
4. Ibid., 154.

Chapter 10 When the Way Comes to an End

1. Diane K. Osbon, ed., *Reflections on the Art of Living: A Joseph Campbell Companion* (New York: HarperPerennial, 1991), 298.

Chapter 11 Put Down the Load and Fly

1. Harold S. Kushner in Simon Wiesenthal, *The Sunflower: On the Possibilities and Limits of Forgiveness*, rev. ed (New York: Schocken Books, 1997), 176, 177.
2. Mark L. Prophet and Elizabeth Clare Prophet, *Saint Germain On Alchemy: Formulas for Self-Transformation* (Corwin Springs: Summit University Press), 296.
3. Charlotte vanOyen Witvliet, Thomas E. Ludwig, Kelly L. Vander Laan, "Granting Forgiveness or Harboring Grudges: Implications for Emotion, Physiology, and Health, *Psychological Science* 12, no. 2 (2002): 117-23; Giacomo Bono and Michael E. McCullough, "Positive Responses to Benefit and Harm: Bringing Forgiveness and Gratitude into Cognitive Psychotherapy," *Journal of Cognitive Psychotherapy* 20, no. 2 (2006); James W. Carson, Francis J. Keefe, Veeraindar Goli, Anne Marie Fras, Thomas R. Lynch, Steven R. Thorp, and Jennifer L. Buechler, "Forgiveness and Chronic Low Back Pain: A Preliminary Study Examining the Relationship of Forgiveness to Pain, Anger, and Psychological Distress," *The Journal of Pain* 6, no. 2 (2005), 84-91.

Chapter 12   Your Inborn Note

1. Henrik Ibsen, *Peer Gynt*, trans. R. Farquharson Sharp, act 5, sc. 3.
2. Teresa of Avila, *The Interior Castle* (London: Fount, 1995), 192.
3. Viktor E. Frankl, *Man's Search for Meaning: An Introduction to Logotherapy*, 3rd ed. (New York: Simon & Schuster, 1984), 145, 113.
4. Thomas Merton, *No Man Is an Island* (San Diego: Harcourt, 1983), 122.

Chapter 13   Walk in Your Own Shoes at Your Own Pace

1. The Teachings of Silvanus in *The Nag Hammadi Library in English*, 390.
2. Luke 17:21; The Gospel of Thomas 3 in *The Nag Hammadi Library in English*, 126.
3. The Gospel of Thomas 70 in Marvin Meyer, trans., *The Gospel of Thomas: The Hidden Sayings of Jesus* (New York: HarperCollins, 1991), 53.
4. Imam Muhammad Al-Ghazali, *The Alchemy of Happiness*, trans. Claud Field.
5. The Bhagavad Gita 3:35 in Juan Mascaro, trans., *The Bhagavad Gita*, 59.
6. All the quotations from Emerson in this chapter are from his essay "Self-Reliance."

Chapter 14   Ever More Magnificent

1. Rabindranath Tagore, *Sadhana: The Realisation of Life* (New York: The Macmillan Company, 1916), 41
2. Thomas Merton, *New Seeds of Contemplation* (New York: New Directions, 1972), 31, 32.
3. The Gospel of Truth in *The Nag Hammadi Library in English*, 47.
4. Abraham H. Maslow, *The Farther Reaches of Human Nature* (New York: Penguin, 1993), 34-35.
5. Marianne Williamson, *A Return to Love* (New York: HarperPerennial, 1996), 191.
6. The Bhagavad Gita 3:8 and 18:48 in Juan Mascaro, trans., *The Bhagavad Gita*, 56, 119.
7. Jonathan Star, trans., *Rumi: In the Arms of the Beloved* (Jeremy P. Tarcher/Putnam: 1997), 70.

Chapter 15   Broadening Your Vision of the Possible

1. Madeleine L'Engle, *A Circle of Quiet* (New York: HarperCollins, 1972), 32.
2. Abraham H. Maslow, *The Farther Reaches of Human Nature*, 176-77.

PATRICIA SPADARO has coauthored six books on personal growth and practical spirituality. Her books have been translated into eighteen languages and are available in over twenty-five countries worldwide. Patricia is also a publishing coach, freelance writer, and executive editor who has helped many successful authors publish and market their works. She lives with her husband in Bozeman, Montana. For more resources, including *Honor Yourself* study guides for reading groups, visit Patricia Spadaro at HowtoHonorYourself.com and PracticalSpirituality.info.